KAY EWING'S COOKING SCHOOL COOKBOOK...

The Final Course

To Lesley -
Merry Christmas -
now your collection
is complete!

Love,
Mom

KAY EWING'S COOKING SCHOOL COOKBOOK...

The Final Course

By
Kay Ewing

DEDICATION

To all of the wonderful cooks who have taken my classes over the past twenty-nine years… thank you!

Ewing, Kay
KAY EWING'S COOKING SCHOOL COOKBOOK...
The Final Course

ISBN 978-0-9643611-6-4

Published by Kay Ewing's Everyday Gourmet
Baton Rouge, Louisiana
2014

CONTENTS

INTRODUCTION

KAY EWING'S COOKING SCHOOL COOKBOOK...THE FINAL COURSE completes my career of 29 years of teaching cooking classes. This is a collection of all the recipes prepared in classes since the publication of A THIRD HELPING in 2005, A SECOND COURSE in 1999 and my first book, KAY EWING'S COOKING SCHOOL COOKBOOK in 1994.

Throughout those many years, I have enjoyed being able to share recipes and techniques with so many wonderful people. What started with a few full participation classes taught in my home, to more classes taught at The Panhandler, and continued to more than I could handle at The Royal Standard....I have had a very rewarding career.

As expected, recipes have gotten much easier to prepare over the years. New food products and better accessibility of products have made cooking a fun experience for everyone.

I hope you will enjoy the cookbook as I have enjoyed teaching so many of you.

Kay Ewing

ASIAN CUISINE

DIM SUM DUMPLINGS
with SWEET & HOT SAUCE

EDAMAME

THAI COCONUT CHICKEN SOUP

SICHUAN PORK

DAN DAN NOODLES

GOOD FORTUNE ICE CREAM DELIGHT

DIM SUM DUMPLINGS

½ cup finely chopped ham
2 Tablespoons chopped green onion
1 cup shredded coleslaw mix
1 Tablespoon oyster sauce
1 Tablespoon soy sauce
1 teaspoon sesame oil
1 Tablespoon cornstarch
32 dumpling or won ton wrappers

Combine ham, green onion, coleslaw mix, oyster sauce, soy sauce, sesame oil and cornstarch. Place about 1 teaspoon filling in the center of each wrapper and moisten the edges with a little water. Bring sides up to meet and pleat edges, pressing together to hold. Arrange dumplings standing and apart from each other in 2 greased bamboo steamer racks, on a wire rack or a vegetable steamer. To cook, place about 1 inch of water in a wok or large skillet and bring to a boil over high heat. Place steamer rack over water and cover. Let steam for about 15 minutes. Serve with Sweet & Hot Sauce.

SWEET & HOT SAUCE

½ cup cider vinegar
½ cup water
¼ cup light brown sugar
¼ cup sugar
¼ cup cornstarch
½ cup pineapple juice
1 Tablespoon soy sauce
1 teaspoon chili oil

Bring vinegar, water, brown sugar and sugar to a boil in a small saucepan over medium heat. Combine cornstarch and pineapple juice together and add to hot mixture. Cook until thickened. Stir in chili oil and soy sauce. Serve warm with Dumplings.

EDAMAME

Frozen soy beans (Edamame)
Salt

Bring a large pot of water to a boil and add frozen soy beans. Cook for 1 minute. Remove and sprinkle with salt. Pop seeds out to eat. Discard the pods.

THAI COCONUT CHICKEN SOUP

1/8 lb. (2 ½ oz) rice noodles
6 cups chicken broth
3 Tablespoons lime juice
1 clove garlic, pressed
2 Tablespoons soy sauce
1 teaspoon chili oil
½ lb. (3) chicken breast tenders
14 oz. unsweetened coconut milk
½ cup shredded carrot
¼ cup chopped green onion
¼ cup chopped parsley
½ cup snow peas

Bring 2 cups of water to a boil and pour over noodles in a bowl. Let soak for about 15 minutes. Drain and cut strands into pieces.

Place broth, lime juice, garlic, soy sauce and chili oil in a large pot and bring to a boil over medium high heat. Add chicken and cook 10 minutes. Remove chicken and shred with a fork. Return to pot with coconut milk, carrots, green onion and parsley. Cook 5 minutes. Stir in snow peas and noodles and cook 5 minutes more.

GOOD FORTUNE ICE CREAM DELIGHT

1 cup Swirled semisweet & white chocolate chips
2 Tablespoons butter
¼ cup vegetable oil
Vanilla ice cream
Fortune cookies

Melt chips and butter in the microwave at half power. Stir until smooth. Add oil and return to microwave to heat until warm. Serve over scoops of vanilla ice cream and garnish with coarsely crushed fortune cookies.

SICHUAN PORK

1 ½ - 2 lbs. pork tenderloin
3 Tablespoons soy sauce
1 Tablespoon rice wine
2 teaspoons sesame oil
½ teaspoon chili oil
1 Tablespoon cornstarch
3 Tablespoons vegetable oil
Chopped green onion for garnish

Trim pork and cut into ¼ inch slices, then cut slices into strips. Mix together soy sauce, rice wine, sesame oil, chili oil and cornstarch with a whisk. Pour over pork and marinate at least 10 minutes or more. Heat oil in a wok or large skillet over medium high heat and stir fry pork until no longer pink, about 5 minutes. Serve over Dan Dan Noodles and garnish with green onion.

DAN DAN NOODLES

1 lb. wide egg noodles
1 cup chicken broth
½ cup tahini (sesame seed paste)
2 Tablespoons oyster sauce
1 Tablespoon rice vinegar
2 teaspoons chili paste

Bring a large pot of salted water to a boil over high heat. Add noodles and cook until tasted done. In the meantime, mix together chicken broth, tahini, oyster sauce, rice vinegar and chili paste until combined. When noodles are done, drain and mix with sauce.

BACK TO BASICS

BLEU CHEESE SALAD

SOUTHWESTERN PASTA JAMBALAYA

PEANUT BUTTER SHEET CAKE

BLEU CHEESE SALAD

1 ½ cups sour cream
¼ cup mayonnaise
1 cup crumbled bleu cheese
1 Tablespoon Worcestershire sauce
½ teaspoon salt
½ teaspoon pepper
2 Tablespoons apple cider vinegar
4 dashes Tabasco
Milk (optional)

Lettuce (mixed greens, romaine, butter, green leaf)
Chopped grape tomatoes
Crumbled, cooked bacon bits

Make dressing by mixing together sour cream, mayonnaise, bleu cheese, Worcestershire, salt, pepper, vinegar and Tabasco. If dressing is too thick, add a little milk until desired consistency. Cover and chill.

Prepare individual salads by tearing lettuce onto plates. Top with dressing and garnish with tomatoes and bacon.

SOUTHWESTERN PASTA JAMBALAYA

1 lb. ground round beef
1 onion, chopped
½ green bell pepper, chopped
1 clove garlic, pressed
¼ cup chopped pork tasso
1 (28 oz) can crushed tomatoes
1 (15 oz) can black beans, rinsed & drained
¼ cup chopped green onion
¼ cup chopped parsley
2 teaspoons cumin
½ teaspoon chipotle chile powder
1 cup frozen corn
Salt & pepper to taste
1 lb. penne pasta
2 cups grated cheddar cheese

Place ground beef in a large pot and cook over medium high heat, until no longer pink. Add onion, bell pepper, garlic and tasso. Sauté for 5 minutes. Add tomatoes, black beans, green onion, parsley, cumin, chipotle chile, corn, salt and pepper. Cover and cook 15 minutes over medium heat, stirring occasionally.

In the meantime, bring a large pot of salted water to a boil. Add pasta and cook until tested done, about 12 minutes. Drain and save about 1 cup of "pasta water". Stir cooked pasta into ground meat mixture to combine. Add cheese and gently stir. Use saved water to moisten pasta, if necessary.

PEANUT BUTTER SHEET CAKE

1 cup butter
½ cup water
½ cup creamy peanut butter
¼ teaspoon salt
2 cups sugar
2 cups flour
2 eggs, lightly beaten
1 cup buttermilk
1 teaspoon baking soda
1 teaspoon vanilla
1 cup Swirled peanut butter & chocolate chips

Preheat oven to 375°. Melt butter and water in a medium saucepan over medium heat. Whisk in peanut butter. Add salt, sugar and flour. In a separate bowl, combine eggs, buttermilk, baking soda and vanilla. Add to butter mixture and stir to combine. Pour into a greased 9 x 13 inch baking pan and sprinkle with 1 cup Swirled chips. Bake about 30 minutes, until tested done. Make icing.

ICING:
½ cup butter
¼ cup creamy peanut butter
2 cups powdered sugar
2 Tablespoons milk
1 teaspoon vanilla
Swirled peanut butter & chocolate chips

Melt butter in a microwave proof bowl. Stir in peanut butter, powdered sugar, milk and vanilla. Spread over warm cake and sprinkle with the remainder of (10 oz) bag of Swirled chips. Let melt and gently smooth out over cake. Cool in pan before serving.

(If Swirled chips are not available, use a mixture of chocolate chips and peanut butter chips.)

BEST OF THE BEST

GORGONZOLA PARADISE SALAD with GLAZED PECANS

SEAFOOD CANNELLONI SEMPLICE

CARAMEL CUP CUSTARD

GORGONZOLA PARADISE SALAD with GLAZED PECANS

¾ cup olive oil
¼ cup Vanilla Fig Balsamic vinegar
¼ teaspoon salt
1/8 teaspoon pepper
Red onion
Sweet red bell pepper
Leaf lettuce
Avocado slices
Gorgonzola cheese

Measure olive oil, vinegar, salt and pepper together and whisk until combined.

Slice red onion and bell pepper very thin (a Mandolin works well). Heat a grill pan over medium high heat and cook onion and bell pepper until lightly grilled.

To serve, make individual salads using leaf lettuce, slices of avocado, grilled red onion and bell pepper and Gorgonzola cheese. Drizzle each salad with dressing. Top with Glazed Pecans.

GLAZED PECANS:
1 Tablespoon butter
1 Tablespoon sugar
1 teaspoon water
1 cup pecan halves

Melt butter in a small skillet over medium heat. Mix in sugar and water, cook until bubbly, then add pecans. Stir constantly for 5 minutes. Pour onto a piece of aluminum foil, separate and cool.

SEAFOOD CANNELLONI SEMPLICE

SEAFOOD FILLING:

¼ cup butter
3 lbs. medium shrimp, peeled
8 oz. sliced mushrooms
1 clove garlic, pressed
1 cup chopped green onion
¼ cup grated Romano cheese
1 teaspoon Cavender's Greek seasoning

Melt butter in a large saucepan over medium high heat. Add shrimp and sauté until pink. Add mushrooms, garlic and green onion and sauté for 5 minutes. Season with cheese and Cavender's. Remove from heat to cool.

CREAM SAUCE:

½ cup butter
½ cup flour
2 ½ cups half & half cream, heated
½ cup grated Romano cheese
¼ teaspoon salt
1/8 teaspoon pepper

Melt butter in a medium saucepan over medium heat. Stir in flour and cook, stirring constantly for 3 minutes. Add warm cream and stir until mixture boils and thickens. Add cheese, salt and pepper. Remove from heat, let cool and add to Seafood Filling. Cool before assembling cannelloni.

TOMATO SAUCE:

2 (28 oz) cans crushed tomatoes
¼ cup sugar
1 teaspoon salt
½ teaspoon pepper
1 teaspoon oregano
1 teaspoon basil

Bring all ingredients to a boil in a saucepan over medium heat. Cover and cook for 10 minutes.

(Continued on next page)

(SEAFOOD CANNELLONI continued)

TO ASSEMBLE:
1 pkg. egg roll wrappers
¼ cup grated Romano cheese
¼ cup chopped parsley

Preheat oven to 375°. Place a layer of tomato sauce into the bottom of 2 large greased baking dishes. Spoon some seafood filling into the middle of an egg roll wrapper and roll up. Place seam side down on tomato sauce. Repeat. Spoon any remaining seafood filling with cream sauce over the top of the cannelloni. Top with some tomato sauce and sprinkle with cheese and parsley. Cover with foil and bake for about 20 minutes, until hot. Serve with additional tomato sauce and cheese, if desired.

CARAMEL CUP CUSTARD

1 ¼ cups sugar
4 eggs
1 (12 oz) can evaporated milk
1 (5 oz) can evaporated milk
¼ cup water
1 ½ teaspoons vanilla

Preheat oven to 350°. Place 1 teaspoon sugar from measured sugar into 8 greased individual ovenproof baking bowls. Place bowls in a large, deep baking pan and bake until sugar becomes light brown, about 15 minutes. Cool slightly.

Beat eggs with a whisk. Mix in sugar, evaporated milk, water and vanilla. Pour evenly into bowls. Very carefully add hot water to the baking pan to come up half way on the sides of the bowls. Bake about 40 minutes or until tested done with a knife.

Remove bowls from pan of water and cool on a wire rack. Cover each bowl with plastic wrap and chill completely before serving.

To serve, run a knife around the custards to loosen. Turn out onto plates or small bowls and let sauce drip over custard.

BEST OF THE BEST

ORANGE ALMOND SALADE

LOUISIANA MEAT PIES with SAUCE PIQUANT

ADOBE CHOCOLATE CAKE

ORANGE ALMOND SALADE

1/3 cup apple cider vinegar
¾ cup sugar
1 teaspoon salt
1 teaspoon dry mustard
1 cup vegetable oil

Leaf lettuce
1 (15 oz) can Mandarin oranges, chilled & drained
1/4 cup chopped green onion
1/4 cup toasted almond slices

Combine vinegar, sugar, salt and dry mustard in a food processor. With the machine running, very slowly add oil through the feed tube until combined and thickened. Chill.

To serve, prepare individual plates of lettuce and top with oranges, green onion, almond slices and drizzle with dressing.

LOUISIANA MEAT PIES

PASTRY:

2 ½ cups flour
1 teaspoon sugar
1 teaspoon salt
1 egg
½ cup very cold butter, cut up
½ cup cold milk

Measure flour, sugar and salt into a food processor. Pulse to combine. Add egg and butter. Pulse just until crumbly. With the machine running, add milk through the feed tube and process just until dough comes together and forms a ball. Remove, wrap in plastic wrap and chill. Triple recipe, separately, in order to use all of the filling.

MEAT FILLING:

1 lb. bulk pork sausage
1 lb. ground round beef
½ cup vegetable oil
½ cup flour
1 onion, chopped
½ green pepper, chopped
½ cup chopped celery
½ cup chopped green onion
1 ½ cups beef broth, warmed
¼ teaspoon sage
¼ teaspoon thyme
¼ cup chopped parsley
½ teaspoon salt
¼ teaspoon pepper
1/8 teaspoon cayenne

Cook sausage in a large skillet or saucepan over medium high heat until no longer pink. Remove and drain on paper towels. Add ground beef to saucepan and cook until no longer pink. Remove and drain on paper towels also. Lower heat to medium and add oil. When oil is heated, stir in flour and cook, stirring constantly, to a medium brown roux, about 10 minutes, lowering the heat as necessary. Add chopped vegetables and sauté until softened, about 5 minutes. Stir in warmed beef broth and seasonings. Add sausage and ground beef and stir to combine. Cook for about 10 minutes, stirring occasionally and skim off any excess grease. Remove from heat and transfer to a baking dish to cool before assembling meat pies.

(Continued on next page)

(Louisiana Meat Pies continued)

TO ASSEMBLE:

1 egg
2 Tablespoons milk

Preheat oven to 375°. Roll out one recipe of dough on a lightly floured surface to about 1/4 inch thick. Cut out 4 inch rounds and roll each circle again to thin out. Place about 2 Tablespoons cooled meat mixture down the center of the circle. Fold over to enclose meat in a crescent shape. Press with fingers to seal. Crimp edges on both sides with tines of a fork. Place on a greased foil lined baking sheet. Repeat assembly of meat pies using the remaining 2 recipes of dough. (Can be covered, refrigerated and baked later.)

Make an egg wash by beating 1 egg with 2 Tablespoons milk. Before baking, brush the top of each meat pie with the egg wash. Bake for about 30 minutes, until golden brown. Serve with Sauce Piquant. (Makes about 2 dozen meat pies)

SAUCE PIQUANT

¼ cup vegetable oil
1 onion, chopped
1 clove garlic, pressed
½ green bell pepper, chopped
2 (10 oz) cans diced Ro-Tel tomatoes & chilies
2 (15 oz) cans tomato sauce
1 teaspoon sugar
¼ teaspoon salt

Heat oil in a medium saucepan over medium heat. Sauté onion, garlic and green pepper until softened, about 5 minutes. Add Ro-Tel tomatoes, tomato sauce, sugar and salt. Bring to a boil, lower heat and simmer for about 20 minutes. Serve with Meat Pies.

ADOBE CHOCOLATE CAKE

1/3 cup butter, softened
1/3 cup light brown sugar
1/3 cup light corn syrup
½ cup chopped pecans

¼ cup butter, softened
1 cup sugar
1 egg
2 oz. unsweetened chocolate, melted
¼ teaspoon salt
1 Tablespoon baking powder
1 teaspoon vanilla
1 ¼ cups flour
¾ cup milk

Vanilla Ice Cream

Preheat oven to 350°. Grease a 9" round cake pan, line with wax paper and grease again.

Cream butter and brown sugar with an electric mixer for 2 minutes, until fluffy. Add corn syrup and pecans. Spread evenly in the bottom of the cake pan.

In the same bowl, cream ¼ cup butter and 1 cup sugar until fluffy, about 2 minutes. Beat in egg and add melted chocolate, salt, baking powder and vanilla. Alternately add flour and milk to batter, beating well. Pour batter over topping, spreading evenly. Place a piece of foil under pan to catch any spillovers.

Bake about 40 minutes, until tested done. Cool in pan 15 minutes. Turn out onto a serving plate, nut side up. Scrape off any nuts that may have stuck to the pan and add to the top of the cake. Can be served warm or at room temperature. Top with a scoop of vanilla ice cream, if desired.

BREAKFAST FOR SUPPER

CREOLE GRILLADES with CREAMY GRITS

SUNDAY NIGHT QUICHE

CROQUE MONSIEUR & CROQUE MADAME

CREOLE GRILLADES with CREAMY GRITS

GRILLADES:

2 – 2 ½ lbs. pork tenderloin
Salt, pepper & flour
¼ cup vegetable oil, divided
1 onion, chopped
½ green bell pepper, chopped
½ cup chopped celery
1 clove garlic, pressed
1 (28 oz) can petite diced tomatoes
½ cup chopped green onion
½ cup chopped parsley
1 cup red wine (Pinot Noir)
1 cup chicken broth
½ teaspoon thyme
1 teaspoon sugar
Salt & pepper to taste
Pinch of cayenne

Prepare pork by trimming off excess fat. Slice pork into ¼ inch slices. Season with salt, pepper and flour. Heat 2 Tablespoons oil in a large saucepan over medium high heat. Add pork and cook 2 minutes on each side, in 2 batches. Remove and add onion, bell pepper, celery and garlic. Sauté for 10 minutes. Add tomatoes, green onion, parsley, wine, broth, seasonings and pork. Bring to a boil and cook, uncovered and maintaining a boil, until reduced and thickened, about 30 minutes. Serve over grits.

CREAMY GRITS:

2 cups water
2 cups chicken broth
1 cup milk
1 cup half & half cream
1 ½ cups quick grits
2 teaspoons salt

Place water, broth, milk and cream in a large saucepan over medium high heat and bring to a boil. Stir constantly while adding salt and grits. Lower heat to medium, cover loosely and cook until grits thicken, stirring occasionally to keep from sticking.

SUNDAY NIGHT QUICHE

BISCUIT CRUST:

1 cup flour
½ teaspoon salt
1 teaspoon sugar
1 ½ teaspoons baking powder
¾ cup heavy cream

Preheat oven to 375°. Mix together all ingredients in a bowl until combined. Roll out on a lightly floured surface to about 12 inches and place inside a greased 9 inch springform pan, to cover the bottom and halfway up the sides of the pan.

FILLING:

½ lb. ground pork sausage
½ cup chopped green onion
1 cup shredded cheddar cheese
4 eggs, lightly beaten
1 cup half & half cream
½ teaspoon salt
¼ teaspoon pepper

Place sausage in a skillet over medium high heat and cook until no longer pink, stirring frequently to break up. Sprinkle over bottom of biscuit crust, along with green onion and cheese. Whisk together eggs, cream, salt and pepper in a small bowl until combined. Carefully pour over ingredients in the crust and bake for about 30 minutes until firm and browned. Let cool 5 - 10 minutes before slicing.

CROQUE MONSIEUR & CROQUE MADAME

SAUCE:
2 Tablespoons butter
3 Tablespoons flour
1 ½ cups milk, warmed
½ teaspoon salt
¼ teaspoon pepper
½ cup grated Romano or Parmesan cheese

CROQUE MONSIEUR:
Oroweat Oatnut Bread
Dijon mustard
Thin sliced or shaved ham
Sliced Swiss cheese
Roma tomatoes, sliced
Romano or Parmesan cheese for garnish

Preheat oven to 400°. Melt butter in a medium saucepan over medium heat. Add flour and cook, stirring constantly, for 2 minutes. Add warm milk and bring to a boil. Stir in salt, pepper and cheese.

Place bread slices on a greased foil lined baking pan. Toast in oven for 2 – 3 minutes, turn and toast other side for 2 – 3 minutes. Top half of bread slices with a light spreading of mustard, 2 – 3 slices of ham and 1 slice of cheese. Top with another slice of toasted bread. Cut in half diagonally. Spoon some sauce on top of sandwiches and top with a slice of tomato and a sprinkle of Romano cheese. Bake for 10 minutes until hot.

CROQUE MADAME:
Egg
Salt & pepper

For each sandwich, cook an egg seasoned with salt and pepper, over easy, in a greased nonstick skillet over medium heat until desired doneness. Place on top of sandwich before serving.

BRUNCH

EGGS FLORENTINE

BUTTERMILK HAM & CHEESE BISCUITS

FRUIT MELANGE with ORANGE CREAM

LEMON BLUEBERRY MUFFINS

SIPPING CHOCOLATE MARTINI

EGGS FLORENTINE

¼ cup butter
¼ cup flour
1 clove garlic, pressed
¾ cup chicken broth, warmed
¾ cup milk, warmed
Salt & pepper to taste

3 (6 oz) bags fresh baby spinach
2 oz. Pepper Jack cheese, cut up
1 cup shredded Cheddar cheese
8 - 10 eggs
Salt & pepper

Melt butter in a large saucepan over medium heat. Add flour and garlic and cook, stirring constantly, for 2 minutes. Stir in warmed broth, milk, salt and pepper. Lower heat and gradually stir in spinach until wilted. Add cheeses and cook, stirring frequently, for 5 minutes.

Preheat oven to 375°. Place a portion of hot creamed spinach in individual greased baking dishes. Leave a spot in the center to place egg. Add egg and season with salt and pepper. Bake about 10 - 15 minutes, until set or cooked to desired doneness. Serve immediately.

BUTTERMILK HAM & CHEESE BISCUITS

2 ½ cups flour
2 Tablespoons sugar
½ teaspoon salt
1 Tablespoon baking powder
¼ teaspoon baking soda
6 Tablespoons cold butter, cut
¾ cup buttermilk
1 cup chopped ham
1 cup shredded Cheddar cheese

Preheat oven to 400°. Measure flour, sugar, salt, baking powder and baking soda into a food processor. Pulse a couple of times to combine. Add butter and pulse until crumbly, about 10 times. With the machine running, pour buttermilk through the feed tube just until dough comes together. Add ham and cheese and briefly mix to combine. Remove and place on a lightly floured surface. Roll out dough into an 8" x 10" rectangle and cut out biscuits into squares. Place on a greased foil lined baking sheet. Bake about 12 - 15 minutes, until golden brown. Makes about 16 – 20 biscuits.

LEMON BLUEBERRY MUFFINS

2 eggs
1 cup sugar
½ cup butter, melted & cooled
1 cup sour cream
½ teaspoon salt
1 Tablespoon baking powder
¼ teaspoon baking soda
1 teaspoon lemon extract
2 cups flour
1 cup frozen blueberries
Sugar for topping

Preheat oven to 375°. Beat eggs with a whisk in a large mixing bowl. Whisk in sugar, butter, sour cream, salt, baking powder, baking soda and lemon extract. Use a spoon to stir in flour until combined. Gently stir in blueberries. Spoon into 48 greased mini muffin cups and sprinkle with sugar. Bake about 12 - 15 minutes, until lightly browned. (Makes 48 mini muffins)

FRUIT MELANGE with ORANGE CREAM

1 pint (2 cups) vanilla ice cream
¼ cup prepared orange juice
¼ teaspoon almond extract
Pineapple chunks, apples, grapes, Mandarin oranges

Place ice cream in a small mixing bowl and stir until melted. Mix in orange juice and almond extract.

Prepare fruit and stir into Orange Cream sauce.

SIPPING CHOCOLATE MARTINI

1 cup half & half cream
6 Tablespoons Bellagio's Sipping Chocolate
2 oz. or more Vodka (optional)

Vigorously whisk together cream, sipping chocolate and vodka. Serve chilled.

FALL FEAST

BLT QUESADILLAS

MOJO PULLED PORK with SALSA VERDE CREMA

COWBOY SLAW

WHITE CHOCOLATE PECAN SHEET CAKE

BLT QUESADILLAS

1 cup mayonnaise
1 Tablespoon chipotle chili paste
12 flour tortillas (fajita size)
12 slices bacon, cooked & diced
1 cup grape tomatoes, sliced
2 cups shredded Colby Jack cheese
Shredded lettuce
Guacamole & salsa for garnish

Preheat oven to 350°. Stir together mayonnaise and chipotle chili paste together until combined. Spread a heaping Tablespoon of mayonnaise mixture on the bottom half of each tortilla. Top each half with crumbled bacon, grape tomatoes, cheese and a little lettuce. Fold other tortilla half over and cut in half. Secure each quarter with a toothpick.

Place on a greased foil lined baking sheet and bake for 5 minutes, until warmed. Serve garnished with a little guacamole and salsa on top of each quesadilla. (Makes 24 quesadillas)

COWBOY SLAW

½ cup olive oil
¼ cup balsamic vinegar
2 Tablespoons lime juice
1 teaspoon salt
¼ teaspoon pepper
1 Tablespoon chipotle chili paste
2 cups frozen corn, thawed
1 (15 oz) can black beans, rinsed
½ cup grape tomatoes, halved
1 lb. coleslaw mix
2 Tablespoons chopped cilantro (optional)

Mix together olive oil, vinegar, lime juice, salt, pepper and chili paste with a whisk until combined. Place all other ingredients in a large bowl and toss with dressing to coat. (Serves 8)

MOJO PULLED PORK with SALSA VERDE CREMA

2 ½ lbs. pork tenderloin
Cavender's Greek seasoning
¼ cup olive oil
Zest of 1 lime and 1 orange
¼ cup lime juice
¼ cup orange juice
1 clove garlic, pressed
½ teaspoon salt
¼ teaspoon pepper
Garnish: chopped parsley (or cilantro), chili powder & toasted tortilla sticks

Preheat oven to 400°. Trim any excess fat from pork and place on a roasting rack over a greased foil lined baking pan. Season all over with Cavender's. Roast for 45 minutes. In the meantime, mix together olive oil, zest, lime juice, orange juice, garlic, salt and pepper with a whisk until combined for Mojo sauce.

Remove pork from oven. Cut tenderloins into 4 inch pieces and pull into shreds with 2 forks. Place in a greased baking dish and cover with Mojo sauce. Return to the oven for 15 minutes.

SALSA VERDE CREMA:
1 cup sour cream
1/3 cup salsa verde
3 Tablespoons lime juice
1 teaspoon salt

Stir together all ingredients until combined.

TOASTED TORTILLA STICKS:
2 flour tortillas
Cooking spray

Cut tortillas into sticks, place on a greased foil lined baking sheet and spray with cooking spray. Toast in a 400° oven until lightly browned, stirring occasionally, for about 10 minutes.

TO ASSEMBLE:

Place a portion of Cowboy Coleslaw in the middle of a plate and surround with Mojo Pulled Pork. Place Salsa Verde Crema in a squeeze bottle and drizzle sauce over entire plate. Garnish the rim of each plate with chopped parsley or cilantro and chili powder. Place a few tortilla strips on top of each serving. (Serves 8)

WHITE CHOCOLATE PECAN SHEET CAKE

1 cup butter
½ cup water
3 oz. white chocolate, chopped
2 cups sugar
2 cups flour
½ teaspoon salt
1 teaspoon baking soda
1 cup buttermilk
2 eggs, lightly beaten
1 teaspoon almond extract
½ cup frozen flaked coconut, thawed

Preheat oven to 375°. Melt butter and water in a large saucepan until boiling. Remove from heat and stir in white chocolate with a whisk until smooth and melted. Whisk in all other ingredients until combined. Pour into a greased 9 x 13 inch baking pan. Bake about 30 minutes, until tested done. Remove and immediately make icing.

ICING:
½ cup butter
1 oz. white chocolate, chopped
2 cups powdered sugar
2 Tablespoons milk
1 cup chopped pecans

Melt butter in the microwave. Remove and stir in white chocolate until smooth and melted. Stir in powdered sugar, milk and pecans. Pour over warm cake and spread gently to cover. Let cool in pan.

FALL FEAST

CREAMY BROCCOLI SOUP
with ROASTED PEPPER COULIS

PORK MEDALLIONS SAUCISSE
& CORNBREAD GÂTEAU

MOLTEN CHOCOLATE CAKES

CREAMY BROCCOLI SOUP

1 lb. broccoli florets, cut
2 medium Yukon Gold potatoes, peeled & sliced thin
¼ cup butter
1 onion, chopped
¼ cup flour
3 cups chicken broth, warmed
1 ½ cups milk, warmed
Salt, pepper & cayenne to taste
1 cup shredded fontina cheese

Cook broccoli and potatoes in a large pot of boiling water until tender, about 10 minutes. Drain.

Melt butter in a large saucepan over medium heat. Add onion and sauté for 5 minutes. Stir in flour and cook, stirring constantly, for 2 minutes. Add warmed broth, milk and seasonings and bring to a boil. Add broccoli and potatoes and purée with a hand held blender or in a food processor. Stir in cheese and taste for seasonings. Serve garnished with Roasted Pepper Coulis.

ROASTED PEPPER COULIS

½ cup roasted red bell pepper, drained
1 teaspoon olive oil
1 teaspoon balsamic vinegar
¼ teaspoon salt
1/8 teaspoon pepper

Measure all ingredients together and purée with a hand held blender or in a food processor. Drizzle over each serving of soup.

PORK MEDALLIONS SAUCISSE

2 – 2 ½ lbs. pork tenderloin
Salt, pepper & balsamic vinegar
2 Tablespoons butter
2 Tablespoons olive oil
1 lb. bulk pork sausage
1 onion, chopped
1 clove garlic, pressed
½ cup flour
¼ cup chopped green onion
¼ cup chopped parsley
4 cups chicken broth, warmed
Salt, pepper & cayenne to taste

Preheat oven to 375°. Trim pork of any excess fat and cut each tenderloin into 8 medallions. Season both sides with salt, pepper & brush with balsamic vinegar. Heat butter and oil in a large saucepan over medium high heat. Add pork in 2 batches and cook until browned on both sides. Remove and place in an ovenproof baking dish. Add sausage to saucepan and cook, stirring to break up, until no longer pink. Add onion and garlic and sauté for 5 minutes. Stir in flour, green onion and parsley and cook, stirring constantly, for 2 minutes. Deglaze pot with broth and bring to a boil. Add seasonings and pour over pork. Bake, uncovered, for about 15 minutes. Serve over Cornbread Gâteau.

CORNBREAD GÂTEAU

½ cup flour
½ cup cornmeal
¼ teaspoon salt
2 teaspoons sugar
1 ½ teaspoons baking powder
1 egg
¾ cup buttermilk
¼ teaspoon baking soda
¼ cup butter, melted & cooled
2 teaspoons chipotle chili paste
1 cup shredded cheddar cheese

Preheat oven to 425°. Measure flour, cornmeal, salt, sugar and baking powder in a mixing bowl and stir to combine. In another bowl, lightly beat egg and stir in buttermilk, baking soda, butter and chipotle chili paste . Add to dry ingredients along with cheese. Stir until mixed and pour into a greased 9 inch round baking pan. Bake about 10 minutes. Cut into rounds to serve and top with Pork Medallions Saucisse.

MOLTEN CHOCOLATE CAKES

½ cup butter
4 oz. semisweet chocolate
1 cup powdered sugar
¼ cup flour
½ teaspoon vanilla
4 eggs, lightly beaten
Vanilla ice cream

Preheat oven to 375°. Melt butter and chocolate in a saucepan over low heat. Whisk in powdered sugar, flour and vanilla. Remove from heat and add eggs and whisk until combined. Divide batter between 8 greased custard cups or small ovenproof bowls.

Place on a baking pan and bake about 8 - 10 minutes. Centers will be loose and sides will rise. Cool 5 minutes. Remove cakes from cups by running a small knife around the edge of each cup and invert into small individual bowls. Top warm cakes with a scoop of vanilla ice cream. Serve immediately.

Cakes can be made ahead and refrigerated before baking. Bake about 5 minutes longer.

FALL FEAST

MEDITERRANEAN SHRIMP REMOULADE

SAVORY BREAD PUDDING

PORK MEDALLIONS CHINOIS with WILTED SPINACH & CHEESE CRISPS

FROZEN MALTED MILK PIE

MEDITERRANEAN SHRIMP REMOULADE

1 ½ lbs. peeled shrimp
3 Tablespoons salt
1 Tablespoon liquid crab boil

1 (14 oz) can artichoke hearts, drained and cut
2 Tablespoons sliced black olives
¼ cup quartered grape tomatoes

1/3 cup vegetable oil
2 Tablespoons cider vinegar
1 Tablespoon paprika
2 teaspoons Old Bay seasoning
1/8 teaspoon cayenne
3 Tablespoons grainy Dijon
¼ cup chopped celery
¼ cup chopped green onion
Crackers

Bring a large pot of water to a boil. Add shrimp, salt and crab boil. Cook about 5 minutes, until tasted done. Drain and cool shrimp. When cool, cut shrimp into bite size pieces and place in a large bowl with artichokes, black olives and tomatoes.

Place all ingredients for remoulade sauce in a food processor and mix until combined and smooth. Toss with shrimp mixture and serve with crackers.

SAVORY BREAD PUDDING

¼ cup butter
1 onion, chopped
1 clove garlic, pressed
½ cup chopped celery
¼ cup chopped green onion
¼ cup chopped parsley
12 slices of soft white bread
½ cup dried cranberries
3 cups milk
1 cup chicken broth
1 teaspoon salt
½ teaspoon pepper
¼ teaspoon cayenne
1 teaspoon poultry seasoning
3 eggs, lightly beaten

Preheat oven to 350°. Melt butter in a large skillet over medium heat. Add onion, garlic and celery and sauté 5 minutes. Stir in green onion and parsley. Tear bread into large pieces into a large greased baking dish. Top with sautéed vegetables and cranberries. Heat milk and broth in the microwave until warm. Whisk in seasonings and eggs. Pour over bread mixture and gently mix in. Bake about 40 – 45 minutes. Let sit to deflate before serving. Cut into squares and top with 2 pork medallions, wilted spinach and cheese crisps.

PORK MEDALLIONS CHINOIS

2 ½ lbs. pork tenderloin, trimmed
Cavender's Greek seasoning
2 Tablespoons butter
2 Tablespoons vegetable oil
1 Tablespoon Teriyaki sauce
1 cup chicken broth
1 Tablespoon sweet Dijon
3 Tablespoons Hot Squeeze
½ teaspoon sesame oil
2 Tablespoons cornstarch mixed with 2 Tablespoons water

Preheat oven to 375°. Cut each pork tenderloin into 8 medallions. Season both sides with Cavender's. Heat butter and oil in a large skillet and brown pork in two batches, about 5 minutes on each side. Place in a large greased baking dish and brush with Teriyaki sauce.

Heat chicken broth in the microwave and mix in mustard, Hot Squeeze chipotle sauce, sesame oil and cornstarch mixture. Pour over pork and place in the oven for about 15 minutes. Serve 2 medallions over a square of bread pudding. Top with wilted spinach and a cheese crisp.

WILTED SPINACH

1 Tablespoon butter
12 – 16 oz. fresh baby spinach
Salt & pepper to taste
1 Tablespoon heavy cream

Melt butter in a large saucepan over medium heat. Gradually stir in spinach until wilted. Add salt, pepper and heavy cream. Cook until most of the liquid has evaporated.

CHEESE CRISPS

Fontina cheese

Use a vegetable peeler to peel thin strips from a block of Fontina cheese. Place strips in a greased non-stick skillet and cook over medium heat until very lightly browned and can be turned with a spatula. Cook lightly on the second side until crispy.

FROZEN MALTED MILK PIE

CRUST:

12 Oreos

2 Tablespoons butter, melted

Crush Oreos in a food processor until smooth. Add butter and mix to combine. Press evenly into the bottom of a greased 9 inch springform pan. Place in freezer.

FILLING:

2 cups malted milk balls, Coarsely crushed

4 cups vanilla ice cream

Place malted milk balls in a food processor and pulse to gently crush into coarse pieces. Place ice cream in a large bowl and stir in crushed malted milk balls. Spread ice cream mixture into crust, cover with foil and freeze until firm.

SAUCE:

½ cup heavy cream
1 cup milk chocolate chips

½ cup chocolate malted milk powder
1 Tablespoon corn syrup
1 teaspoon vanilla

Heat cream and malted milk powder together over medium heat until bubbly. Stir in chocolate chips, corn syrup and vanilla and cook 3 minutes, stirring frequently. Drizzle over slices of pie. Can be made ahead, stored in the refrigerator and reheated in the microwave.

FALL FEAST

ROASTED GARLIC SOUP

POULET AU VIN

ALMOND RICE PILAF

CHOCOLATE PECAN TART

ROASTED GARLIC SOUP

2 heads (bulbs) of garlic
½ teaspoon olive oil

¼ cup butter
½ onion, chopped
¼ cup flour

2 medium white potatoes (1 lb), peeled & chopped
4 cups chicken broth, warmed
Salt & pepper to taste
1 cup half & half cream
Chopped parsley for garnish

Preheat oven to 325°. Cut a small slice off the top of the whole garlic heads to expose garlic cloves. Place in a garlic roaster or small baking dish, drizzle with olive oil, cover and roast for 30 minutes. Remove cover and roast 30 minutes more. When cool enough to handle, squeeze garlic pulp from peel.

Melt butter in a large saucepan over medium heat. Add onion and sauté for 5 minutes. Add flour and cook, stirring constantly, for 2 minutes. Add roasted garlic, potatoes, chicken broth, salt and pepper. Bring to a boil, cover and lower heat. Cook for 15 minutes, stirring occasionally. Purée soup with an immersion blender or in a food processor until smooth. Stir in cream and heat thoroughly. Taste for seasonings. Serve garnished with a little chopped parsley.

POULET AU VIN

16 – 18 chicken breast tenders
Salt, pepper & flour
¼ cup butter
2 Tablespoons vegetable oil
1 onion, chopped
1 cup chopped ham
2 cloves garlic, pressed
1 (8 oz) pkg. sliced mushrooms
½ cup chopped green onion
¼ cup flour
½ cup dry white wine
2 cups chicken broth
Salt, pepper & cayenne

Preheat oven to 350°. Season chicken with salt and pepper and dust with flour. Melt butter and oil in a large skillet or sauté pan over medium high heat. Add half the chicken and cook 5 minutes on each side. Remove and place in a large ovenproof baking dish. Repeat with the remaining chicken.

Lower heat to medium and sauté onion, ham and garlic for 5 minutes. Add mushrooms and green onion. Stir in flour and cook, stirring constantly, for 2 minutes. Deglaze the pan with the wine and broth. Add seasonings. Bring to a boil and pour sauce over chicken. Bake, uncovered, for 15 minutes. (Can be made ahead and reheated, covered, in the oven.)

ALMOND RICE PILAF

¼ cup butter
½ onion, chopped
2 cups rice
½ cup almond slices
½ cup chopped parsley
2 cups chicken broth
2 cups water
Salt & pepper to taste

Grease a medium size saucepan with cooking spray and melt butter over medium heat. Add onion and sauté for 5 minutes. Stir in rice, almonds and parsley. Cook 2 minutes, stirring frequently. Add chicken broth, water, salt and pepper. Turn heat to high and bring to a boil. Cook until most of the liquid has evaporated. Turn off heat, cover and let steam for about 20 minutes.

CHOCOLATE PECAN TART

CRUST:

1 ½ cups flour
2 Tablespoons sugar
¾ cup cold butter, cut up
3 Tablespoons ice water

Preheat oven to 400°. Place flour, sugar and butter in a food processor fitted with the metal blade. Pulse briefly to combine. With machine running, slowly add water through the feed tube and mix just until dough forms a ball. Remove dough and pat with fingers into a greased 9 inch fluted tart pan with a removable bottom. Press dough out to cover bottom and up the sides of the pan. Cover with a piece of foil, greased on the bottom, directly on top of dough and fill with dried beans or pie weights. Also, place a piece of foil under the tart pan to catch any drippings. Freeze for 10 minutes. Bake at 400° for 25 minutes. Carefully remove foil with weights and bake another 10 minutes. Make filling.

FILLING:

1 ½ cups coarsely chopped pecans
1 cup heavy cream
¾ cup sugar

Place all ingredients in a small saucepan, stirring to blend. Bring to a boil over medium heat. Cook 5 minutes, without stirring. Pour into crust and bake 15 minutes. Remove and cool 15 minutes. Make glaze.

GLAZE:

4 oz. German's Sweet Chocolate
2 Tablespoons butter
1 Tablespoon water

Melt all ingredients slowly in a small saucepan over low heat, until smooth. Spread evenly over tart.

Chill in the refrigerator until chocolate is set before serving. Store in the refrigerator. To serve, remove tart from refrigerator for 10 - 15 minutes before serving.

Garnish with a sprinkling of powdered sugar on each piece just before serving.

FALL FEAST

CREAMY ARTICHOKE SOUP with HONEY CROISSANTS

CLASSIC RISOTTO

PORK TENDERLOIN SANTORINI

CHOCOLATE PANNA COTTA with CHERRY COULIS

CREAMY ARTICHOKE SOUP

¼ cup butter
½ onion, chopped
½ cup chopped celery
¼ cup flour
4 cups chicken broth, warmed
2 (14 oz) cans artichoke hearts, drained
¼ teaspoon thyme
1/8 teaspoon cayenne
Salt & pepper to taste
Chopped parsley for garnish

Melt butter in a large saucepan over medium heat. Add onion and celery and sauté for 5 minutes. Stir in flour and cook, stirring constantly, for 3 minutes. Add broth, artichokes, thyme and cayenne. Taste before adding salt and pepper. Bring mixture to a boil. Lower heat, cover and cook 15 minutes.

Purée soup with a hand held blender or in a food processor until smooth. Pour through a fine mesh strainer. Return to heat and serve warm with a garnish of parsley. Serve with Honey Croissants on the side.

HONEY CROISSANTS:
Baked croissants
Honey

Preheat oven to 375°. Place croissants on a greased foil lined baking sheet. Drizzle with a little honey and bake about 5 minutes, until warm. Serve with soup.

CLASSIC RISOTTO

¼ cup butter
½ onion, chopped
1½ cups Arborio rice
4 cups hot chicken broth
Salt & pepper to taste
2 Tablespoons chopped parsley

Melt butter in a medium saucepan over medium heat. Add onion and sauté for 5 minutes. Stir in rice to coat and add 2/3 cup hot broth. Cook, stirring frequently, until broth is almost absorbed. Keep adding 1/3 cup chicken broth at a time, stirring frequently until absorbed, before adding more. Cook until all the broth is absorbed and the risotto becomes thick and creamy, about 25 – 30 minutes. Stir constantly towards the end of cooking, so risotto doesn't stick. Taste for doneness and seasoning. Stir in salt, pepper and parsley. Turn off heat, cover and let steam for about 15 minutes

PORK TENDERLOIN SANTORINI

2 - 2 ½ lbs. pork tenderloin
Cavender's Greek seasoning
¼ cup olive oil
Flour
½ cup chopped green onion
1 clove garlic, pressed
2 cups chicken broth, warmed
2 Tablespoons Vanilla Fig Balsamic Vinegar
1 Tablespoon Dijon mustard
2 Tablespoons chopped sun dried tomatoes
2 Tablespoons chopped Kalamata black olives
2 Tablespoons capers
¼ cup chopped parsley
Feta cheese & toasted pine nuts for garnish

Preheat oven to 375º. Trim pork tenderloins and cut each into 8 medallions. Season both sides lightly with Cavender's. Heat oil in a large skillet over medium high heat. Sprinkle half the pork with flour and cook 5 minutes. Flour top side, turn over and cook 5 minutes more. Place in a large baking dish. Repeat with remaining pork. Add green onion and garlic to skillet and cook 1 minute. Stir in remaining ingredients and cook until bubbly. Pour sauce over pork and bake in oven for 15 minutes. Serve over Risotto and sprinkle with feta cheese and a few pine nuts for garnish.

CHOCOLATE PANNA COTTA

2 pkgs. unflavored gelatin
¼ cup milk
2 cups heavy cream
½ cup powdered sugar
½ cup Bellagio Sipping Chocolate
1 teaspoon vanilla
1 cup milk
Whipped cream

Stir gelatin into milk and let stand. Place cream and powdered sugar in a 4 cup glass measurer and whisk to combine. Microwave just until boiling, about 2 minutes. Whisk in Sipping Chocolate powder until smooth. Add gelatin and stir to dissolve. Stir in vanilla and milk and whisk until smooth. Pour into 8 (4 oz) greased custard cups or molds. Chill until firm, about 1 hour.

To serve, unmold and turn out onto dessert plates or shallow bowls. Garnish with whipped cream and serve with Cherry Coulis.

CHERRY COULIS:

1 (15 oz) can dark sweet cherries
¼ cup powdered sugar
1 Tablespoon prepared orange juice

Drain cherries and place in a food processor. Add powdered sugar and orange juice. Process until smooth. Pour through a fine mesh strainer.

FALL FEAST

GOLDEN TOMATO SALADE with WARM GOAT CHEESE

PLANTATION PORK with ROUX GRAVY

SOUTHERN CORNBREAD DRESSING

DOUBLE SAUCED ICE CREAM BALLS

GOLDEN TOMATO SALADE with WARM GOAT CHEESE

½ cup olive oil
2 Tablespoons lemon juice
1 teaspoon Dijon mustard
½ teaspoon sugar
½ teaspoon salt
½ teaspoon pepper

Butter lettuce
Golden tomatoes, halved
Roasted sunflower kernels
Goat cheese
Sweet onion cane sugar
Salt & pepper
Vanilla Fig Balsamic Vinegar

Make dressing by whisking together all ingredients until combined.

Tear lettuce and place in a large bowl. Toss with dressing. Place on individual salad plates and garnish with tomatoes and sunflower seeds.

Slice goat cheese and sprinkle with sweet onion cane sugar (by FlavorStorm), salt and pepper. Place a small skillet, sprayed with Pam, over medium heat. Add cheese and heat just until slightly warmed, about 20 seconds, carefully flip over and heat other side. Place cheese on each salade, drizzle with a tiny amount of vinegar and serve immediately.

SOUTHERN CORNBREAD DRESSING

CORNBREAD:

1 cup flour
1 cup yellow cornmeal
½ teaspoon salt
1 Tablespoon sugar
1 Tablespoon baking powder
½ cup butter, melted
2 eggs
1 ½ cups buttermilk
½ teaspoon baking soda

Preheat oven to 425°. Place all dry ingredients in a mixing bowl and stir to combine. Melt butter and allow to cool slightly. Lightly beat eggs in another mixing bowl and add buttermilk and baking soda. Stir in butter and mix in dry ingredients. Pour into a greased 9 x 13 inch baking pan and bake 15 minutes.

DRESSING:

¼ cup butter
1 onion, chopped
1 clove garlic, pressed
½ cup chopped celery
¼ green bell pepper, chopped
¼ cup chopped green onion
¼ cup chopped parsley
1 ½ cups chicken broth
½ teaspoon salt
½ teaspoon pepper
1/8 teaspoon cayenne
2 teaspoons poultry seasoning
1 cup dried cranberries

Preheat oven to 350°. Melt butter in a large skillet or saucepan over medium heat. Sauté onion, garlic, celery and bell pepper for 10 minutes. Stir in green onion and parsley.

Coarsely crumble cornbread in a large bowl and add vegetables. Mix in broth, seasonings and cranberries. Place in a large greased baking dish, cover with foil and bake about 20 minutes. To reheat, moisten with a little water or broth.

ROUX GRAVY

½ cup butter
½ cup flour
1 onion, chopped
1 clove garlic, pressed
½ cup chopped celery
¼ green bell pepper, chopped
1 ½ cups hot chicken broth
1 cup hot beef broth
½ teaspoon Kitchen Bouquet
½ teaspoon poultry seasoning
¼ teaspoon dry mustard
Salt, pepper & cayenne to taste
¼ cup chopped green onion
¼ cup chopped parsley

Place butter in a large saucepan over medium heat. When butter is melted and hot, stir in flour and cook, stirring constantly, for about 15 minutes until golden brown. Add vegetables and cook 5 minutes, stirring constantly. Add hot broths and seasonings, bring to a boil and cook 30 minutes, stirring occasionally and lowering the heat as necessary. Taste for seasonings, add green onion and parsley and pour over pork.

PLANTATION PORK with ROUX GRAVY

2 – 2 ½ lbs. pork tenderloin
Salt, pepper, onion sugar & flour
2 Tablespoons vegetable oil
2 Tablespoons butter
4 oz. Baby Bella mushrooms, chopped

Preheat oven to 350°. Trim fat from pork and cut each tenderloin into 8 medallions. Season with salt, pepper and sweet onion cane sugar (by FlavorStorm) on each side.

Heat oil and butter in a large skillet over medium high heat. Flour one side of 8 medallions and place flour side down in skillet. Cook 5 minutes, flour and flip. Cook 5 minutes more. Remove to a large baking dish and repeat with remaining medallions. Add mushrooms to skillet and sauté about 2 minutes. Pour over pork and cover with Roux Gravy. Place in the oven to cook for about 10 minutes.

DOUBLE SAUCED ICE CREAM BALLS

CHOCOLATE SAUCE:

¼ cup butter
2 Tablespoons vegetable oil
½ cup semisweet chocolate chips
½ teaspoon vanilla

Place all ingredients in a microwave proof bowl and heat on half power until melted. Stir until smooth. Cool before serving. Can be made ahead and stored in the refrigerator and reheated when needed.

CARAMEL SAUCE:

¼ cup butter
½ cup light brown sugar
1 Tablespoon light corn syrup
1/3 cup heavy cream
½ teaspoon vanilla

Place all ingredients in a microwave proof bowl and heat on half power until melted. Stir until smooth. Cool before serving. Can be made ahead and stored in the refrigerator and reheated when needed.

ICE CREAM BALLS:

Vanilla Ice Cream
Chopped pecans, toasted
Heath Toffee Bits
Cyprus Flake salt

Make scoops of ice cream shaped into balls. Roll in pecans and Heath bits to coat. Return to freezer until firm. (Can be made ahead)

To serve, place an ice cream ball in a small bowl, spoon one side with Chocolate Sauce and the other side with Caramel Sauce. Top with a very tiny sprinkle of salt. Serve immediately.

FIRESIDE SUPPER

FIG BALSAMIC & PEAR SALADE with NAPA CROSTINI

BRAISED CHICKEN STROGANOFF & PASTA CARBONARA

WHITE CHOCOLATE PEACH BREAD PUDDING

FIG BALSAMIC & PEAR SALADE

DRESSING:
¼ cup Vanilla Fig Balsamic vinegar
¾ cup olive oil
1 teaspoon sugar
½ teaspoon salt
¼ teaspoon pepper
1 teaspoon Dijon mustard

SALADE:
Butter lettuce or spring mix
Bosc pears, sliced very thin
Crumbled bleu cheese
or Gorgonzola
Toasted almonds

Make dressing by measuring all ingredients together and whisking until combined. Cover and chill.

Make individual salads by tearing lettuce on each plate. Leave peel on pears, wash, core and cut in half. Cut very thin with a knife or on a mandoline. Place a few slices of pear on each salad. Drizzle with dressing and garnish with crumbled bleu cheese and toasted almonds.

NAPA CROSTINI

French bread baguettes

Pear Fig Jam

Preheat oven to 350°. Slice French bread into thin slices. Lay on a foil lined baking sheet and toast in oven until lightly browned and crispy on both sides, about 10 minutes. Spread each slice with a small amount of Pear Fig Jam and return to oven to heat, about 2 minutes. Serve with Fig Balsamic & Pear Salade.

BRAISED CHICKEN STROGANOFF

8 boneless skinless chicken thighs
Salt & pepper
¼ cup butter, divided
1 onion, quartered & sliced thin
8 oz. sliced mushrooms
1 cup dry white wine (Chardonnay)
1 cup sour cream
1 Tablespoon Dijon mustard
1 Tablespoon tomato paste
2 Tablespoons Worcestershire
1 Tablespoon chopped sun dried tomatoes
1 teaspoon paprika
½ teaspoon salt
¼ teaspoon pepper
Chopped parsley for garnish

Preheat oven to 350°. Remove any excess fat from chicken and season with salt & pepper on both sides. Melt half the butter in a large saucepan or skillet over medium high heat. Add half the chicken and brown on each side. Remove and place in a large greased baking dish. Repeat with remaining butter and chicken. After removing chicken, add onion to the saucepan, lower heat to medium and sauté, stirring occasionally, for 5 minutes. Add mushrooms and cook 3 minutes more. Deglaze with wine and bring to a boil. In the meantime, mix sour cream, Dijon, tomato paste, Worcestershire, sun dried tomatoes, paprika, salt & pepper in a small bowl with a whisk until combined. Stir into wine mixture until combined and heated. Pour sauce over chicken, cover with foil and bake 1 hour. Can be made ahead and reheated in the oven. Serve over Pasta Carbonara and garnish with chopped parsley. (Serves 8)

PASTA CARBONARA

1 lb. fettuccine pasta
½ cup heavy cream
2 Tablespoons butter
½ teaspoon salt
¼ teaspoon pepper
¼ cup crumbled cooked bacon
¼ cup chopped parsley

Bring a large pot of salted water to a boil and add pasta. Cook until tasted done. Heat cream, butter, salt & pepper in the microwave until hot and butter is melted. Drain pasta and toss with cream mixture, bacon and parsley. Stir until combined and let stand a few minutes for pasta to absorb the sauce. Serve topped with Chicken Strogranoff. (Serves 8)

WHITE CHOCOLATE PEACH BREAD PUDDING

12 slices of soft white bread
1 lb. frozen peaches, thawed & cut
1 cup heavy cream
2 cups milk
¼ cup butter, cut up
2 oz. white chocolate, chopped
3 eggs
1 ½ cups sugar
1 teaspoon almond extract

Preheat oven to 350°. Tear bread into medium pieces in a large greased baking dish. Sprinkle peaches over bread. Heat cream, milk and butter in the microwave until hot and butter melts. Stir in chopped white chocolate until melted and pour over bread and peaches. In a separate bowl, whisk together eggs, sugar and almond extract. Pour over bread mixture and gently stir in. Bake about 45 minutes. Serve topped with White Chocolate Sauce. (Serves 8 – 10)

WHITE CHOCOLATE SAUCE:
½ cup heavy cream
4 oz. white chocolate, chopped

Heat cream in the microwave until boiling. Whisk in white chocolate until combined. Drizzle over bread pudding.

FIRESIDE SUPPER

DELI TOMATO SOUP

OLD FASHIONED
CREAMED CHICKEN
with SOUTHERN STYLE BISCUITS

MARBLED NUTELLA
CHEESECAKE

DELI TOMATO SOUP

¼ cup butter
1 small onion, chopped
2 Tablespoons flour
2 (14.5 oz) cans petite diced tomatoes
¼ teaspoon salt
¼ teaspoon pepper
¼ teaspoon baking soda
¼ teaspoon thyme
½ cup prepared orange juice
1 cup chicken broth
¼ cup heavy cream
Drizzle of cream for garnish

Melt butter in a large saucepan over medium heat. Add onion and sauté for 5 minutes. Add flour and cook, stirring constantly, for 2 minutes. Stir in tomatoes, salt, pepper, baking soda, thyme, orange juice and chicken broth. Bring to a boil and cook 15 minutes, stirring occasionally. Purée with a hand held blender or in a food processor. Return to heat and stir in cream until heated through. Garnish each serving with a drizzle of cream.

OLD FASHIONED CREAMED CHICKEN with SOUTHERN STYLE BISCUITS

14 chicken breast tenders
Salt & pepper
¼ cup butter
1 onion, chopped
½ cup chopped celery
1 cup chopped carrots
½ cup flour
3 cups chicken broth, warmed
2 cups milk, warmed
1 cup frozen green peas
¼ cup chopped green onion
¼ cup chopped parsley
¼ teaspoon poultry seasoning
¼ teaspoon cayenne pepper
Salt & pepper to taste

Cut chicken tenders into bite size pieces and season with salt and pepper. Melt butter in a large dutch oven or stockpot over medium high heat. Add chicken and cook, stirring occasionally, until no longer pink. Stir in onion, celery and carrots. Cook, stirring occasionally, for 5 minutes. Lower heat to medium, add flour and stir constantly for 2 minutes. Stir in all remaining ingredients. Taste before adding any salt & pepper. Bring to a boil and cook for 10 minutes, stirring occasionally. Add a little water if mixture is too thick. Serve over split biscuits.

SOUTHERN STYLE BISCUITS

2 cups flour
1 teaspoon salt
2 teaspoons sugar
1 Tablespoon baking powder
1½ cups heavy cream

Preheat oven to 425°. Stir dry ingredients together in a large bowl. Add heavy cream and stir until mixture holds together. Turn out on a floured surface and knead slightly. Gently roll out to ½" thickness. Cut with a 3" round cutter. Gather any excess dough to finish cutting biscuits. Place on a greased foil lined baking sheet and bake 15 minutes until golden brown. (Makes 8 - 9)

MARBLED NUTELLA CHEESECAKE

CRUST:

24 Biscoff cookies
¼ cup butter, cut up
2 Tablespoons brown sugar

Preheat oven to 350º. Place cookies in a food processor and crush. Add butter and sugar and mix until combined. Prepare a 9 inch springform pan by covering the inside bottom with foil. Clamp side of pan evenly onto the bottom and cover the outside bottom with another piece of foil, to catch any drippings. Grease with cooking spray. Press crust evenly over the bottom of the pan and bake crust for 10 minutes.

FILLING:

3 (8 oz) pkgs. cream cheese
1 cup sugar
2 teaspoons vanilla
3 eggs
¼ cup heavy cream
½ cup Nutella (chocolate hazelnut spread)

Wipe out bowl and blade of food processor with a paper towel. Cut up cream cheese and place in food processor with sugar, vanilla, eggs and cream and mix to combine. Remove 1 cup batter. Pour remaining batter over crust. Return 1 cup batter to food processor and add Nutella. Mix to combine. Spoon over top of cheesecake and use a small knife to gently marbleize. Bake 50 minutes. Remove from oven and run a thin spatula or knife around the inside edge of the pan to help minimize cracking. Cool completely on a wire rack before refrigerating. Chill at least 8 hours or more, until completely firm before serving. Sprinkle each slice with powdered sugar, if desired.

FIRESIDE SUPPER

CROOKNECK SQUASH SOUP

HOMEMADE PIZZA: GREEK style & NEW ORLEANS style

LOLLIPOP BROWNIES

CROOKNECK SQUASH SOUP

2 Tablespoons butter
1 onion, chopped
1 clove garlic, pressed
5 small or 3 large yellow squash (1 ½ lbs.), quartered & coarsely chopped
3 cups chicken broth
1 (8 oz) can tomato sauce
½ teaspoon sugar
¼ teaspoon thyme
¼ teaspoon oregano
Salt & pepper to taste
Smidgen of cayenne pepper
Grated Romano cheese
Chiffonade of fresh spinach or chopped parsley

Melt butter in a large saucepan over medium heat. Add onion & garlic and sauté 5 minutes. Add squash, broth, tomato sauce, sugar, thyme, oregano, salt, pepper & cayenne. Bring to a boil, cover and cook for 30 minutes. Taste for seasonings and serve garnished with cheese and spinach.

HOMEMADE PIZZA

4 cups flour
2 pkgs. Rapid Rise Yeast
2 teaspoons sugar
2 teaspoons salt
1 ½ cups warm water (120 – 130°)
2 Tablespoons olive oil

Preheat oven to 425°. Place flour, yeast, sugar & salt in a food processor fitted with the metal blade and pulse to combine. Measure water and check temperature. Add oil to water and with machine running, pour steadily through the feed tube until the dough comes together. Process for 1 minute to knead dough. Keep the cover on the work bowl and let dough rest for 15 minutes or longer. Remove dough to a lightly floured surface and shape into a ball. Flatten slightly and divide in half. Cut each half into 6 pieces. Roll out each piece into about a 6 inch circle and place pizzas on a greased foil lined baking pan. Place toppings on individual pizzas and put pan on the bottom rack of the oven to bake about 10 minutes, until bottom of crusts have browned. Repeat baking until all pizzas are cooked. Makes 12 individual pizzas.

Pizza dough can be made ahead and kept in a Ziploc in the refrigerator for up to 1 week. Let come to room temperature before rolling out dough (about 2 – 3 hours).

GREEK style:
Prepared Hummus
Golden grape tomatoes, sliced
Shredded fresh spinach
Crumbled feta cheese

NEW ORLEANS style:
Prepared Olive Mix
Thin sliced ham, chopped
Hard salami, chopped
Provolone cheese, chopped

LOLLIPOP BROWNIES

½ cup butter
2 oz. unsweetened chocolate
1 cup sugar
2 eggs
¼ teaspoon salt
½ teaspoon vanilla
½ cup flour
½ cup finely chopped pecans

Preheat oven to 325°. Place butter and chocolate in a small saucepan over low heat, stirring until melted. Remove from heat and whisk in sugar. Mix in eggs, one at a time, and add salt and vanilla. Use a spatula to stir in flour and pecans. Pour into a greased 8 inch round cake pan. Bake about 30 minutes, until tested done. Let cool completely in pan and cut with a small 2" round cookie cutter into 12 rounds. Place a lollipop stick into the side of each brownie and put on a cooling rack to ice.

CHOCOLATE ICING:
2/3 cup powdered sugar
2 teaspoons cocoa
About 1 Tablespoon water

Place powdered sugar and cocoa in a small bowl. Stir in about 1 Tablespoon of water until a thick, spreading consistency. Use a small spatula to spread icing on top of each brownie.

WHITE ICING:
¼ cup powdered sugar
About 1 – 1 ½ teaspoons water

Place powdered sugar in a small bowl and add enough water to obtain a thick drizzling consistency. Pour into a small Ziploc and snip off a tiny corner to drizzle icing over each brownie. Let stand until icing sets up and dries.

GIFTS OF FOOD

TOFFEE COFFEE CAKE MUFFINS

GREEK FETA CRUMBLE

ANISE BISCOTTINI

PEANUT BUTTER PRETZEL TRUFFLES

STRAWBERRY CHIPOTLE JAM

GORGONZOLA TORTILLA BITES

TOFFEE COFFEE CAKE MUFFINS

MIX:
2 cups flour
1 cup sugar
½ teaspoon salt
¼ teaspoon baking soda
1 Tablespoon baking powder
2 teaspoons cinnamon
1 cup Heath toffee bits
½ cup white baking chips
½ cup chopped pecans

TO BAKE:
2 eggs
½ cup butter, melted & cooled
1 cup sour cream
1 teaspoon vanilla
Extra sugar

Measure all ingredients in a large mixing bowl and stir to combine. Place in a quart size Ziploc bag.

To bake muffins, preheat oven to 375°. Beat 2 eggs with a whisk in a large mixing bowl. Mix in ½ cup cooled melted butter, 1 cup sour cream and 1 teaspoon vanilla. Stir in muffin mix until combined. Batter will be thick. Fill 12 greased regular size muffin cups with batter and top with a little extra sugar. Bake about 20 minutes until tested done. (Give directions and a list of ingredients for baking along with the muffin mix.)

GREEK FETA CRUMBLE

¼ cup olive oil
1 clove garlic, pressed
¼ teaspoon salt
¼ teaspoon pepper
¼ teaspoon oregano
Zest of 1 lemon
2 Tablespoons lemon juice

2 cups crumbled feta cheese
½ cup sliced grape tomatoes
¼ cup sliced green olives
¼ cup sliced black olives
1 Tablespoon chopped parsley
2 Tablespoons toasted pine nuts
Warm pita bread cut into eighths

Mix together olive oil, garlic, salt, pepper, oregano, lemon zest and lemon juice with a whisk until combined. Place feta cheese in a large dish or shallow bowl. Top with a layer of tomatoes, green olives, black olives, parsley and pine nuts. Drizzle dressing over cheese mixture. Serve with warm pita bread.

ANISE BISCOTTINI

½ cup butter, softened
1 cup sugar
3 eggs
2 Tablespoons anise extract
1 Tablespoon baking powder
3 cups flour

ICING:
2 cups powdered sugar
2 – 2 ½ Tablespoons hot water
Decorative sprinkles

Preheat oven to 375°. Beat butter and sugar with an electric mixer for about 2 minutes. Add 3 eggs, one at a time, until combined. Mix in anise extract, baking powder and flour. Divide dough into 3 parts on a large greased baking sheet. Shape each piece into a long log, about 1 ½ inches wide (use cooking spray on hands to easily shape dough). Bake about 20 minutes, until lightly browned. Remove from oven and let cool for 5 minutes. Cut each log into ½ inch slices with a serrated knife and lay slices on their side. Return to oven for about 8 – 10 minutes, until lightly toasted. Let cool on pan and stand cookies upright before icing.

Make icing by mixing powdered sugar and enough water to form a drizzling consistency. Pour into a plastic squeeze bottle or Ziploc and drizzle over cookies and immediately top with sprinkles before icing sets. (Makes about 6 dozen small Biscotti)

PEANUT BUTTER PRETZEL TRUFFLES

2 cups crushed pretzels (6 heaping cups tiny twists)
1 cup creamy peanut butter
7 oz. marshmallow crème
2 squares chocolate almond bark
1 square vanilla almond bark

Crush pretzels in a food processor until finely crushed. Place peanut butter and marshmallow crème in a large glass bowl and microwave until melted, about 1 minute. Add crushed pretzels and stir to completely moisten. Shape about a Tablespoon of pretzel mixture for each truffle into a solid ball, with hands sprayed with cooking spray, and place on a sheet of wax paper.

Carefully melt chocolate almond bark in the microwave over low heat. Place in a Ziploc, cut a small corner of the bag and drizzle over truffles. Melt vanilla almond bark in microwave, place in a Ziploc, cut a small corner of the bag and drizzle over truffles. Let stand until dry. (Makes about 3 dozen)

STRAWBERRY CHIPOTLE JAM

16 oz. frozen sweetened sliced strawberries, thawed
1 teaspoon balsamic vinegar
2 teaspoons chipotle chili paste

Thoroughly drain juice from thawed strawberries and coarsely chop. Mix with balsamic vinegar and chipotle paste. Store in the refrigerator. (Makes 1 half pint.) Serve with Gorgonzola Tortilla Bites.

GORGONZOLA TORTILLA BITES

8 oz. cream cheese, softened
½ cup crumbled Gorgonzola cheese
1/8 teaspoon salt
6 flour tortillas (fajita size)
Finely chopped pecans, toasted

Mix cream cheese, Gorgonzola and salt together with a hand held mixer until smooth. Divide between 6 tortillas and spread to cover. Sprinkle with chopped pecans. Roll up tightly, cover and chill. Cut each tortilla roll into ½ inch slices with a serrated knife and lay slices on their side to serve. If made ahead, cover with a damp paper towel and plastic wrap to keep from drying out in the refrigerator. Serve with Strawberry Chipotle Jam.

GIFTS OF FOOD

MARVELOUS MARBLE CAN CAKES

WHITE CHOCOLATE SNOWFLAKES

TIGER TAILS

MUFFALETTA TORTA

BLEU CHEESE PÂTÉ

MARVELOUS MARBLE CAN CAKES

1 cup butter, softened
2 ¼ cups sugar
4 eggs
2 teaspoons vanilla
½ teaspoon salt
1 ½ teaspoons baking powder
½ teaspoon baking soda
3 cups flour
1 cup buttermilk
¼ cup cocoa
2 teaspoons almond extract

Preheat oven to 350°. Beat butter and sugar in a large mixing bowl with an electric mixer for about 3 minutes, until creamy and smooth. Add eggs, one at a time, until combined. Mix in vanilla, salt, baking powder and baking soda. Alternately mix in flour and buttermilk until combined, scraping bowl down occasionally. Remove about 2 cups of batter to a small bowl and stir in cocoa. To the remaining white batter, add the almond extract.

Grease 8 (15 – 16 oz) cans with cooking spray. Place on a foil lined baking sheet. Place about a spoonful of white batter in each can, then add a smaller spoonful of chocolate batter, until all the batter is divided fairly evenly between the 8 cans. Run a knife gently through the batters to create a marble swirl. Bake about 30 - 35 minutes, until tested done. Cool in cans for 10 minutes. Turn out and place upright on a rack to cool completely before glazing.

CHOCOLATE GLAZE:
2 cups powdered sugar
3 Tablespoons cocoa
½ teaspoon vanilla
About 3 Tablespoons hot water

Stir ingredients together, adding just enough water to get a drizzling consistency. Place in a Ziploc bag, snip off a small corner and drizzle glaze over the top of the upright cakes, letting glaze fall over the sides of the cakes. Let dry slightly.

WHITE GLAZE:
1 cup powdered sugar
About 1- 2 Tablespoons hot water

Stir powdered sugar and enough water to form a drizzling consistency. Place in a Ziploc bag, snip off a small corner and drizzle over chocolate glaze. Let dry before storing.

WHITE CHOCOLATE SNOWFLAKES

6 oz. white chocolate
1 cup butter, softened
1 cup powdered sugar
¼ teaspoon salt
¼ cup cornstarch
1 teaspoon vanilla
2 cups flour
Powdered sugar for garnish

Preheat oven to 350°. Finely chop white chocolate in a food processor or with a mezzaluna. Set aside. Beat butter and powdered sugar together with an electric mixer for about 2 minutes, until creamy. Gradually add salt, cornstarch, vanilla, flour and white chocolate, mixing until combined. Roll out half of the dough between plastic wrap, in a 2 gallon Ziploc or in a pie crust maker to about 1/8" – 1/4" thickness. Cut cookies out with a snowflake cutter and place cookies on a greased foil lined baking sheet. (Chill dough slightly if cut cookies are difficult to remove) Bake about 15 minutes, until lightly browned. Cool on sheets. Repeat with remaining dough. Sprinkle with powdered sugar when cool. (Makes about 4 dozen cookies.)

TIGER TAILS

1 (14 oz) bag caramels
1 Tablespoon water
1 (12 oz) bag Pretzel Rods
3 (2 oz) squares chocolate almond bark
3 (2 oz) squares vanilla almond bark

Unwrap caramels and place caramels and water in a microwave proof bowl and heat carefully in the microwave, until melted and smooth. (Can also be placed in a double boiler to melt.) Use a silicone pastry brush to coat pretzel rods with a light coat of caramel over ¾ of pretzel, leaving a handle. Place on well greased foil lined baking sheets. Chill until set. Loosen gently with a flat spatula.

Place chocolate almond bark in a microwave proof bowl and heat carefully until melted and smooth. Put in a quart size Ziploc and snip off a small corner to drizzle chocolate lengthwise over pretzel rods. Chill until set. Place vanilla almond bark in a microwave proof bowl and heat carefully until melted and smooth. Put in a quart size Ziploc and snip off a small corner to drizzle lengthwise over pretzel rods. Chill until set. Store at room temperature. Makes about 3 dozen.

MUFFALETTA TORTA

2 (8 oz) pkgs. cream cheese, cut up
2 Tablespoons butter, cut up
¼ teaspoon pepper
1 cup grated sharp provolone cheese
½ cup olive salad mix
½ cup chopped ham
½ cup chopped hard salami
Parsley for garnish

Place cream cheese, butter, pepper and provolone cheese in a food processor. Mix until combined and smooth. Line a 3 cup size round bowl with foil and grease with cooking spray. Layer the following ingredients in order: olive salad mix, 1/3 cream cheese mixture, chopped ham, 1/3 cream cheese mixture, chopped salami and 1/3 cream cheese mixture. Use a small spatula greased with cooking spray to spread cream cheese mixture easily over other ingredients without mixing. Cover and chill until firm. Turn uncovered bowl upside down on a serving plate and remove foil very gently. Garnish torta with parsley and serve with crackers.

BLEU CHEESE PÂTÉ

8 oz. cream cheese, cut up
¼ cup butter, cut up
1 cup crumbled bleu cheese
¼ teaspoon cayenne
1/3 cup dried cranberries
2 Tablespoons chopped toasted pecans
1/3 cup crumbled cooked bacon
1 Tablespoon chopped parsley

Place cream cheese, butter, bleu cheese and cayenne in a food processor. Mix until smooth. Divide mixture in half in 2 separate bowls. Stir cranberries in one half and top with pecans. Add bacon to the other half and top with parsley. Serve with crackers.

GIFTS OF FOOD

APPLE DAPPLE COFFEE CAKE MIX

PEANUT BUTTER BLONDIES

CHOCOLATE MINT TOFFEE

ASIAN CHICKEN SALAD TORTA

ASIAGO ONION CRUMBLE

APPLE DAPPLE COFFEE CAKE MIX

MIX:
1 cup sugar
2 cups flour
½ teaspoon salt
1 teaspoon baking powder
1 teaspoon baking soda

CRUMB TOPPING:
½ cup light brown sugar
½ cup chopped pecans
1 teaspoon cinnamon

TO MAKE:
½ cup butter, melted
2 eggs
1 cup sour cream
1 teaspoon vanilla
1 medium Gala apple, peeled, sliced & chopped

Prepare mix by measuring ingredients and stirring together. Place in a plastic bag. Prepare crumb topping by measuring ingredients and stirring together. Place in a small Ziploc bag and add to plastic bag with dry mix and seal bag tightly. Give mix with an apple and include a list of ingredients and instructions on how to make.

To make, preheat oven to 350°. Melt butter in the microwave and let cool. Whisk eggs in a large mixing bowl. Add sour cream, melted butter and vanilla. Whisk to combine. Peel, slice and chop apple and stir into batter. Add dry mix and stir to combine. Spread into a greased 9 x 13 inch baking pan. Sprinkle crumb topping over batter. Bake 30 minutes. Let cool in pan and cut into squares to serve.

PEANUT BUTTER BLONDIES

¾ cup butter
½ cup crunchy peanut butter
2 cups light brown sugar
2 eggs
1 teaspoon vanilla
½ teaspoon salt
1 teaspoon baking powder
¼ teaspoon baking soda
2 cups flour
1 cup peanut butter swirl chips

Preheat oven to 350°. Melt butter and place in a large mixing bowl. Whisk in peanut butter, brown sugar, eggs and vanilla. Stir in salt, baking powder, baking soda, flour and chips. Spread into a greased 9 x 13 inch baking pan Bake 25 minutes. Cool in pan. Make chocolate icing.

CHOCOLATE ICING:
1 cup powdered sugar
1 Tablespoon cocoa
½ teaspoon vanilla
1 ½ - 2 Tablespoons hot water

Measure ingredients together in a small bowl with enough water to make a drizzling consistency. Pour into a Ziploc bag, cut off a tiny corner and drizzle icing over blondies. Let set up to dry and cut into bars. (Makes 24 bars)

CHOCOLATE MINT TOFFEE

35 saltine crackers
½ cup butter
1 cup light brown sugar
1 (10 oz) bag Andes Crème de Menthe baking chips

Preheat oven to 350°. Place crackers in a single even layer in a large greased foil lined baking pan (jelly roll size, 15 ½ x 10 ½ x 1). Stir together butter and brown sugar in a small saucepan over medium heat. Bring to a boil and cook 3 minutes, stirring occasionally. Drizzle over crackers to cover completely. Handle with care as mixture is extremely hot. Bake 5 minutes, until bubbly. Sprinkle baking chips over crackers and let cool. Chill in the freezer for 10 minutes, remove and score crackers with a knife to make for easier cutting when firm. Cut into squares or break into uneven pieces. Store either in the refrigerator or at room temperature.

ASIAN CHICKEN SALAD TORTA

1 lb. chicken breast tenders
Salt & pepper
1 teaspoon Teriyaki sauce
½ cup chopped celery
2 Tablespoons mayonnaise
2 Tablespoons sweet Dijon mustard
2 Tablespoons Hot Squeeze
1 teaspoon sesame oil
¼ cup crumbled feta cheese
1 (11 oz) can Mandarin oranges
½ cup green grapes, halved
½ cup dried cranberries
2 Tablespoons sliced almonds
½ cup chow mein noodles

Season chicken with salt & pepper on both sides. Place in a stove top grill pan or skillet over medium high heat and cook 5 minutes on each side. Remove from heat and brush with Teriyaki and let cool. Cut chicken and place in the food processor with celery, mayonnaise, mustard, Hot Squeeze sweet chipotle sauce and sesame oil. Mix until combined and smooth. Place on a platter and top with a layer of feta cheese. Drain Mandarin oranges and place over feta. Place a row of grape halves on top of oranges, all around the outside edge. Place cranberries in the middle. Sprinkle with almonds and place chow mein noodles around the edges of the platter. Serve with crackers.

ASIAGO ONION CRUMBLE

1 Tablespoon butter
½ onion, chopped, about 1 cup
1 teaspoon light brown sugar

8 oz. Asiago cheese

½ cup olive oil
3 Tablespoons Vanilla Fig Balsamic Vinegar
¼ teaspoon salt
¼ teaspoon pepper

Melt butter in a skillet over medium heat. Add onion and sauté 10 minutes, stirring occasionally, until caramelized. Stir in brown sugar. Let cool.

Cut cheese into pieces and place in a food processor. Pulse until crumbly. In a separate bowl, mix olive oil, vinegar, salt and pepper together with a whisk until combined.

To serve, place onions on a plate, top with cheese and pour vinaigrette over all. Serve with Pizza crackers.

PIZZA CRACKERS:

1 pkg. refrigerated pizza crust dough
1 teaspoon olive oil
Cavender's Greek seasoning

Preheat oven to 400°. Lay out dough and cut into 2 inch squares. Brush with a little olive oil and sprinkle with Cavender's. Bake about 12 minutes, until lightly browned.

GIFTS OF FOOD

BANANA PEANUT BUTTER MUFFINS

TEX MEX CHICKEN WINGS

GREEK FETA DIP

BULLSEYES

CHOCOLATE WHITE CHOCOLATE CHIP COOKIES

BANANA PEANUT BUTTER MUFFINS

1 egg
¾ cup sugar
3 ripe bananas, mashed
1/3 cup butter, melted
½ teaspoon salt
1 teaspoon baking powder
1 teaspoon baking soda
1 teaspoon vanilla
1 ½ cups flour
1 cup peanut butter chips

Preheat oven to 350°. Beat egg with a whisk in a large mixing bowl. Whisk in sugar, bananas, melted butter, salt, baking powder, baking soda and vanilla. Stir in flour and peanut butter chips. Line a 12 cup muffin tin with paper liners and spray with cooking spray. Fill each cup with batter and sprinkle with topping.

TOPPING:
1/3 cup light brown sugar
1 Tablespoon flour
1 Tablespoon butter, softened
¼ cup finely chopped pecans

Mix together all ingredients in a small bowl until combined. Sprinkle on top of muffins and bake 20 minutes.

TEX MEX CHICKEN WINGS

24-30 chicken wing pieces
¼ cup butter, melted
1 teaspoon salt
½ teaspoon pepper
1 Tablespoon cumin
2 Tablespoons chili powder
1 teaspoon chipotle chili pepper powder
Hot Squeeze Sweet Chipotle Sauce

Preheat oven to 425°. Arrange chicken wings on a greased foil lined baking pan and brush lightly with melted butter on one side. Mix together all seasoning ingredients and sprinkle on chicken wings. Turn wings over and brush with remaining butter and sprinkle with seasonings. Bake for 40 minutes. Brush with Hot Squeeze sweet chipotle sauce and serve with Baja Cream.

BAJA CREAM:
1 cup sour cream
Zest of a lime
¼ cup lime juice
½ teaspoon salt
½ teaspoon pepper

Mix together all ingredients and serve with chicken wings.

GREEK FETA DIP

1 (8 oz) pkg. cream cheese, cut up
1 cup crumbled feta cheese
1 clove garlic, pressed
½ teaspoon Cavender's seasoning
1/8 teaspoon cayenne
2 Tablespoons lemon juice
1 cucumber, peeled & chopped
1 cup chopped grape tomatoes
¼ cup chopped parsley
¼ cup sliced black olives

Place cream cheese, feta cheese, garlic, Cavender's, cayenne and lemon juice in a food processor and mix until combined and smooth. Spread dip on a plate and garnish with a layer of cucumber, tomatoes, parsley and olives. Serve with pita chips.

BULLSEYES

1 (10 oz) bag peanut butter chips
1 (14 oz) can sweetened condensed milk
½ cup creamy peanut butter
Malted milk balls
Chocolate almond bark

Place peanut butter chips and condensed milk in a small saucepan over medium heat and stir until melted and smooth. Stir in peanut butter. Pour into an 8 or 9 inch baking dish and chill for easier handling.

Scoop out a small amount of peanut butter mixture and wrap around a malted milk ball. Place on a wax paper lined dish and repeat until all the peanut butter mixture is used. Place in the refrigerator to chill.

Melt 2 squares of chocolate almond bark very carefully in the microwave on low power. Pour into a Ziploc and snip off a tiny corner. Drizzle in a bullseye pattern on each piece of candy. Makes about 6 dozen. Can be stored in the refrigerator or at room temperature.

CHOCOLATE WHITE CHOCOLATE CHIP COOKIES

1 cup butter, softened
¾ cup sugar
¾ cup light brown sugar
2 eggs
1 teaspoon baking soda
1 teaspoon hot water
¼ teaspoon salt
1 teaspoon vanilla
½ cup cocoa
1 ¾ cups flour
1 cup white baking chips
½ cup finely chopped pecans
Powdered sugar

Preheat oven to 350º. Cream together butter and sugars in a large mixing bowl with an electric mixer for 2 minutes. Beat in eggs. Mix baking soda with hot water and add to the dough. Mix in salt, vanilla, cocoa, flour, chips and pecans. Chill batter for easier handling.

Use a teaspoon to measure out dough and spray hands with cooking spray to form into balls. Place each ball of dough on a greased foil lined baking sheet and bake about 12 minutes. Cool on sheets. When cooled, sprinkle with powdered sugar. (Makes about 8 dozen cookies)

GIFTS OF FOOD

ULTIMATE CARAMEL POPCORN

SYMPHONY OATMEAL COOKIES

PBPB's
(Peanut Butter Pretzel Bites)

PEPPER JELLY CHEESECAKE

MEATBALLS MEXICANO

BLT DEVILED EGGS

ULTIMATE CARAMEL POPCORN

4 qts. popped corn (½ cup kernels)
1 cup light brown sugar
½ cup light corn syrup
½ cup butter
¼ teaspoon baking soda
¼ teaspoon vanilla
½ cup whole almonds
½ cup cashews
2 squares chocolate almond bark
2 squares vanilla almond bark

Preheat oven to 225°. Place popped corn in a large greased baking pan and remove any unpopped kernels. In a small saucepan over medium heat, combine brown sugar, corn syrup and butter. Stir until melted and bring to a boil. Lower the heat to low and let boil for 5 minutes, stirring occasionally. Remove from heat and stir in soda, vanilla, almonds and cashews. Immediately pour over popcorn and mix well, using two greased wooden spoons. Bake for 1 hour, stirring every 15 minutes.

Carefully melt chocolate almond bark in the microwave using half power and place in a small Ziploc bag. Snip off a tiny corner and drizzle over caramel popcorn. Repeat with vanilla almond bark. Let cool until hardened. Makes 6 small bags of caramel corn.

SYMPHONY OATMEAL COOKIES

¾ cup sugar
1 cup light brown sugar
1 cup butter, melted
1 teaspoon vanilla extract
2 eggs
½ teaspoon salt
1 teaspoon baking soda
2 cups flour
2 cups quick cooking rolled oats
1 (6.8 oz) Symphony candy bar, coarsely chopped
Powdered sugar

Preheat oven to 375º. In a large bowl, stir together sugar, brown sugar, butter and vanilla with a whisk. Add 2 eggs and whisk to combine. Mix in salt and baking soda. Use a spoon to stir in flour and oats until combined. Gently stir in chopped Symphony bar. Use a small ice cream scoop to place cookies on 4 greased foil lined baking sheets. Bake 10 minutes. Let cool on sheet and sprinkle with powdered sugar when cool. (Makes about 6 dozen)

PBPB's

(Peanut Butter Pretzel Bites)

5 squares chocolate almond bark
50 peanut butter pretzel nuggets
6 squares vanilla almond bark
50 peanut butter pretzel nuggets

Melt chocolate almond bark carefully in the microwave using half power. Dip pretzel nuggets, one at a time, in chocolate until coated. Remove with tongs and place on a wax paper lined baking pan. Let stand until hardened.

Melt vanilla almond bark in another bowl and dip pretzel nuggets, one at a time, until coated. Remove and place on another wax paper lined baking pan.

Place remaining melted almond bark into 2 separate Ziplocs. Snip off a tiny corner and drizzle white almond bark over chocolate covered nuggets. Drizzle chocolate almond bark over vanilla covered nuggets. Let stand until hardened.

PEPPER JELLY CHEESECAKE

CRUST:

1/3 cup plain breadcrumbs
1/3 cup pecan halves
1 Tablespoon butter, cut up

Preheat oven to 375°. Mix all ingredients together in the food processer. Press into a greased 7 inch springform pan. Cover outside of pan with foil. Bake about 8 minutes.

FILLING:

1 (8 oz) pkg. cream cheese, cut up
2 Tablespoons hot pepper jelly
¼ teaspoon salt
1 cup shredded cheddar cheese
1 egg

Mix all ingredients in the food processor and pour over crust. Bake about 25 minutes until firm. Cool at least 30 minutes before serving. Can be served warm or cold.

GARNISH:

Chopped parsley
Tomato rose
Crackers

Sprinkle top of cheesecake with chopped parsley and place a tomato rose in the center. Serve with crackers.

MEATBALLS MEXICANO

1 lb. ground round beef
2 Tablespoons Hot Squeeze
1 cup plain breadcrumbs
2 slices plain white bread
1 teaspoon salt
½ teaspoon pepper
2 eggs, lightly beaten
¼ cup chopped green onion
¼ cup chopped parsley or cilantro
1 clove garlic, pressed

Place ground beef, Hot Squeeze Sweet Chipotle Sauce and breadcrumbs in a large bowl and stir to combine. Soak white bread in a little water and squeeze with hands. Tear into small pieces and add to beef. Mix in salt, pepper, eggs, green onion, parsley and garlic until combined. Use a small ice cream scoop to place meatballs on a greased foil lined baking pan. Roll each meatball with hands to round out. Preheat broiler until hot. Broil 5 minutes, turn meatballs over and broil 3 minutes more. (Makes about 5 dozen cocktail size meatballs)

SALSA:
1 (14.5 oz) can petite diced tomatoes
1 (4.5 oz) can chopped green chiles
2 Tablespoons lime juice
½ teaspoon salt
½ teaspoon cumin
¼ teaspoon sugar
2 teaspoons chopped jalapeño

Stir together all ingredients until combined. Warm in the microwave and pour over meatballs. Serve with toothpicks.

BLT DEVILED EGGS

1 dozen eggs
¼ cup mayonnaise
¼ cup sour cream
1/8 teaspoon salt
¼ teaspoon pepper
1 teaspoon Dijon mustard
½ cup bacon bits
Grape tomatoes and lettuce

Place eggs in a large saucepan and cover with about an inch of water. Place on high heat, start timer for 20 minutes and let boil. Remove from heat, drain and cover with cold water. Peel eggs and cut in half. Remove yolks and place in a small bowl. Mash yolks with mayonnaise, sour cream, salt, pepper, Dijon mustard and bacon bits. Use a small ice cream scoop to place yolk mixture into egg white halves. Garnish with a slice of grape tomato and a small chiffonade of lettuce

GIFTS OF FOOD

PEPPERED HAM & CHEESE PÂTÉ

SISTER'S SLIDERS with SPECIAL SAUCE

BEA'S HOT FUDGE SAUCE

SWEET GINGER CRISPS

RUBY RED CUPCAKES

PEPPERED HAM & CHEESE PÂTÉ

3 cups finely chopped ham
8 oz. cream cheese, cut up
3 Tablespoons pepper jelly
1 cup shredded sharp cheddar cheese
Chopped parsley & chopped roasted red bell peppers for garnish
Pita chips or crackers

Place ham, cream cheese, pepper jelly and cheddar cheese in a food processor and mix until combined and smooth. Place mixture in a greased 7 inch springform, bottom lined with foil. Refrigerate until very cold.

To serve, remove pâté from the springform pan and place on a platter. Garnish with parsley and peppers sprinkled on top. Serve with pita chips or crackers.

SISTER'S SLIDERS

1 ¼ lbs. ground round beef
½ teaspoon Cavender's
¼ teaspoon pepper
1 Tablespoon Dijon mustard
1 Tablespoon Balsamic vinegar
Sister Shubert's Parkerhouse Rolls
Sliced dill pickles

Preheat broiler. Mix together ground round, Cavender's, pepper, mustard and vinegar. Shape into 16 small patties. Broil for about 5 minutes.

Bake rolls according to package directions and slice in half. Spread special sauce on both sides of each roll, top with a meat patty and a dill pickle slice and skewer together with a toothpick.

SPECIAL SAUCE:
1/3 cup mayonnaise
1 Tablespoon ketchup
1 Tablespoon yellow mustard
¼ teaspoon paprika

Mix together all ingredients until combined.

BEA'S HOT FUDGE SAUCE

2 oz. unsweetened chocolate
½ cup water
¼ cup sugar
1 (14 oz) can sweetened condensed milk

Heat chocolate and water in a small saucepan over low heat, stirring constantly, until chocolate is melted. Add sugar and condensed milk and cook, stirring occasionally, until sauce comes to a boil and thickens, about 15 minutes. Cool and store in the refrigerator. Reheat amounts as needed in the microwave before serving over vanilla ice cream.

SWEET GINGER CRISPS

1 cup butter, softened
1 cup light brown sugar
1 egg
1/3 cup molasses
1 teaspoon ground cinnamon
1 teaspoon ground ginger
½ teaspoon ground cloves
¼ teaspoon salt
2 teaspoons baking soda
2 ¼ cups flour
Sanding sugar

Preheat oven to 350°. Cream butter and sugar with an electric mixer for 3 minutes. Add egg until blended. Mix in molasses, cinnamon, ginger, cloves, salt and baking soda. Add flour until combined. Chill dough about 10 minutes in the freezer. Use a small scoop to shape cookies and place on a greased foil lined baking sheet. Sprinkle with sugar. Bake one sheet at a time, keeping dough chilled, between batches. Bake for 15 minutes, until browned. Let cool on sheets until crispy and cooled. Makes about 5 – 5 ½ dozen cookies.

RUBY RED CUPCAKES

CAKE:

½ cup butter, softened
1 ½ cups sugar
2 eggs
2 Tablespoons cocoa
1 oz. bottle red food coloring
1 teaspoon salt
1 teaspoon baking soda
2 teaspoons vanilla
1 Tablespoon white vinegar
2 ¼ cups flour
1 cup buttermilk
Mini marshmallows

Preheat oven to 350°. Beat butter and sugar with an electric mixer until light and fluffy, about 5 minutes. Add eggs, one at a time, and beat until combined. Add cocoa and red food coloring and very slowly mix into batter. Mix in salt, baking soda, vanilla and vinegar. Alternately mix in flour and buttermilk, blending well.

Line 24 muffin tin cups with paper liners and spray with Pam. Place about 5 mini marshmallows in the bottom of each cup. Use a cookie scoop to distribute batter over the marshmallows. Bake about 15 minutes, until tested done. Tilt in the pans to cool before icing.

ICING:

¾ cup butter, softened
2 Tablespoons flour
2 ½ cups powdered sugar
½ teaspoon vanilla extract
¼ teaspoon almond extract
1 Tablespoon milk
Decorative sprinkles

Beat butter with an electric mixer until smooth. Mix in flour, powdered sugar, vanilla, almond and milk until combined. Spread on each cupcake and immediately top with sprinkles.

GIFTS OF FOOD

FETA CUCUMBER BITES

ASIAN CHICKEN WINGS

LEMON PISTACHIO BISCOTTI

PEANUT BUTTER CRUNCHERS

FUDGE TRUFFLES

FETA CUCUMBER BITES

2 English hothouse cucumbers
8 oz. cream cheese, softened
1 cup crumbled feta cheese
2 Tablespoons lemon juice
½ teaspoon salt
¼ teaspoon pepper
Dash of cayenne pepper

GARNISH:
Capers
Golden tomato slivers
Roasted red pepper slivers
Black olive slices
Stuffed green olive slices
Red grape tomato slivers

Peel off alternating strips of cucumber and cut in half crosswise, then lengthwise. Remove seeds from cucumber with a spoon. Mix together cream cheese, feta cheese, lemon juice, salt, pepper & cayenne in a small bowl until combined. Spread filling into cucumbers and cut into ½" slices. Garnish each slice with either capers, tomato slivers, red pepper or olive slices. Store in the refrigerator.

ASIAN CHICKEN WINGS

24 - 30 chicken wings
¼ cup butter, melted
2 Tablespoons soy sauce
2 teaspoons sesame oil
1 teaspoon chili oil
Salt & pepper

DIPPING SAUCE:
1 cup sugar
½ cup water
½ cup cider vinegar
2 Tablespoons pepper jelly

Preheat oven to 425°. Arrange chicken wings on a greased foil lined baking pan. Mix together melted butter, soy sauce, sesame oil & chili oil. Brush on one side of wings and season with salt & pepper. Turn over and brush and season the other side. Bake 40 minutes. Serve with sauce.

Make sauce by combining sugar, water & vinegar in a small saucepan over medium heat. Bring to a boil and cook about 20 minutes. Stir in pepper jelly. Serve with wings.

LEMON PISTACHIO BISCOTTI

½ cup butter, softened
1 cup sugar
3 eggs
Zest of a lemon
2 teaspoons lemon extract
¼ teaspoon salt
1 Tablespoon baking powder
3 cups flour
1 cup pistachios

ICING:
1 cup powdered sugar
1 – 1 ½ Tablespoons lemon juice
1 drop yellow food coloring

Preheat oven to 350°. Beat butter and sugar with an electric mixer for 2 minutes. Mix in eggs, lemon zest, lemon extract, salt, baking powder and flour until combined. Stir in pistachios.

Shape into 2 logs (2 ½ x 15 inches) on a greased foil lined baking sheet. (Spray hands with Pam to shape logs). Bake for 25 minutes. Remove and cool for 5 minutes. Cut logs into ¾" slices with a serrated knife and turn slices on their sides. Bake again for 10 minutes, until lightly toasted. Cool in pan.

Make icing by mixing powdered sugar, lemon juice and food coloring until smooth. Pour into a Ziploc bag and snip off a tiny corner off of one edge or use a squeeze bottle to drizzle icing over biscotti in a wavy pattern. Let icing dry before storing. (Makes about 3 dozen)

PEANUT BUTTER CRUNCHERS

½ cup butter, softened
½ cup crunchy peanut butter
½ cup sugar
½ cup light brown sugar
1 egg
1 teaspoon vanilla
¼ teaspoon salt
½ teaspoon baking soda
½ teaspoon baking powder
1 ¼ cups flour
1 cup peanut butter chips
Sanding sugar

Preheat oven to 350°. Cream butter and peanut butter for 2 minutes with an electric mixer. Add sugars and mix until combined. Add egg and vanilla. Mix in salt, baking soda, baking powder and flour. Stir in chips. (Chill dough briefly, if too soft.) Use a small scoop to place cookies on 2 greased foil lined baking sheets. Flatten each cookie with the tines of a fork in one direction. Sprinkle with sanding sugar and bake about 12 – 15 minutes, until golden brown. Cool on sheets. (Makes about 4 ½ dozen cookies)

FUDGE TRUFFLES

1 (14 oz) can sweetened condensed milk
2 cups semisweet or bittersweet chocolate chips
1 (13 oz) jar Nutella
1 teaspoon vanilla
1 cup white baking chips
½ teaspoon almond extract
Cyprus Flake salt

Measure 1 cup sweetened condensed milk, chocolate chips, Nutella and vanilla in a 4 cup glass bowl. Heat in the microwave on half power until smooth, about 2 minutes. Stir until combined.

In a 2 cup glass measurer, place remaining condensed milk, white baking chips and almond extract. Heat in the microwave at half power for about 1 minute. Stir until combined.

Use a small scoop to measure chocolate mixture, place in hand to flatten slightly. Add about ¼ teaspoon white mixture to the center and wrap chocolate around the white center while rolling into a ball. Sprinkle with a tiny bit of sea salt.

Store covered at room temperature. (Makes about 5 dozen)

GIFTS OF FOOD

MEDITERRANEAN
BAKED FETA

FIESTA MONKEY BREAD

MAMA MIA'S
BUTTERMILK POUND CAKE

LOLLIPOP BLONDIES

LEMON FIDDLESTICKS

MEDITERRANEAN BAKED FETA

1 cup crumbled feta cheese
1 Tablespoon arugula pesto
1 Tablespoon lemon juice
1 Tablespoon olive oil
Golden or red grape tomatoes, sliced
Fresh ground pepper
Pita chips

Preheat oven to 375°. In a small ovenproof bowl or dish, combine feta cheese with pesto, lemon juice and olive oil. Cover with foil and bake for 25 minutes. Top with sliced tomatoes, fresh ground pepper and serve with pita chips.

FIESTA MONKEY BREAD

2 (16 oz) cans refrigerated Grands Biscuits
½ cup butter
1 cup prepared salsa
1 (4.5 oz) can chopped green chiles
1 Tablespoon chili powder
2 teaspoons cumin
2 cups shredded cheddar cheese
Prepared guacamole

Preheat oven to 375°. Cut one can of biscuits into fourths. Place in a bundt pan sprayed liberally with Pam. Place butter in a large microwave proof bowl and heat in the microwave until melted. Remove and add salsa, green chiles, chili powder and cumin. Spoon half of mixture over biscuits and top with 1 cup of cheese. Repeat with remaining can of biscuits, top with butter mixture and finish with cheese. Bake for 25 minutes. Let cool in pan for 10 minutes before turning out. Serve with guacamole.

MAMA MIA'S BUTTERMILK POUND CAKE

1 cup butter, softened
2 cups sugar
5 egg yolks
1 cup buttermilk
1 teaspoon vanilla extract
1 teaspoon almond extract
¼ teaspoon baking soda
1 teaspoon baking powder
3 cups flour
5 egg whites
1 cup sugar

Preheat oven to 375º. Beat butter and 2 cups sugar with an electric mixer for 4 minutes, until creamy. Add egg yolks, one at a time, until combined. Mix in buttermilk, vanilla and almond (batter will look curdled). Add baking soda, baking powder and flour and mix until combined.

In a separate bowl, beat egg whites until soft peaks form. Slowly add 1 cup sugar, while beating until stiff peaks form. Stir a couple of spoonfuls of egg whites into the batter to lighten it. Then gently fold egg white mixture into batter, a spoonful at a time, until combined.

Line 8 mini loaf pans with wax paper and spray with Pam. Carefully spoon batter into pans and place on a baking sheet for an easy transfer to the oven. Bake for 35 minutes, until tested done. Cool in pans 5 minutes and turn out to cool completely on a rack and remove wax paper. When cooled, sprinkle with powdered sugar. (Can be baked in a greased tube pan, lined with wax paper, for about 60 – 65 minutes)

LOLLIPOP BLONDIES

¾ cup butter
2 cups light brown sugar
2 eggs
1 teaspoon almond extract
1 teaspoon salt
¼ teaspoon baking soda
1 teaspoon baking powder
2 cups flour
1 cup white baking chips
1 cup dried cranberries
2 squares vanilla almond bark

Preheat oven to 350°. Melt butter in a large glass bowl in the microwave. Whisk in brown sugar, eggs, almond, salt, baking soda and baking powder. Stir in flour, chips and dried cranberries. Pour into a greased 9 x 13 inch baking pan and bake for 25 minutes, until tested done. Let cool in the pan. Use a small round cookie cutter to cut cookies out.

Carefully melt almond bark in the microwave on half power until smooth. Dip the end of a lollipop stick in almond bark and place into the side of each cookie. Place remaining melted almond bark in a small Ziploc, snip off a tiny corner and drizzle a design on each cookie. Let dry completely before wrapping.

LEMON FIDDLESTICKS

1 (16 oz) bag Rold Gold thin pretzel sticks
4 squares vanilla almond bark
1 teaspoon lemon extract
1 cup powdered sugar

Place pretzels in a greased foil baking pan. Carefully melt almond bark in the microwave on half power until smooth. Stir in lemon extract. Pour over pretzels and toss to coat completely. Add powdered sugar and gently stir to coat. Let dry before storing.

ITALIAN CUISINE

RIBOLLITA TUSCAN SOUP

STROMBOLIOS

ITALIAN SAUSAGE, VEGETABLE & TORTELLINI TIMBALE with CREAMY TOMATO VODKA SAUCE

CHOCOLATE BANANA ANGEL PANINI

RIBOLLITA TUSCAN SOUP

2 Tablespoons olive oil
1 onion, chopped
1 clove garlic, pressed
1 (14.5 oz) can petite diced tomatoes
4 cups warm chicken broth
2 (15.8 oz) cans Great Northern beans, rinsed & drained
3 cups shredded cabbage
Salt & pepper to taste
Italian bread slices, toasted
Prepared Pesto
Grated Romano cheese

Heat oil in a large pot over medium heat. Add onion and garlic and sauté until tender, about 5 minutes. Stir in tomatoes, broth and beans. Bring to a boil and add cabbage, salt and pepper. Cover and cook 10 minutes. Taste for seasonings.

To serve, spread slices of toasted Italian bread with a little pesto. Place in individual serving bowls and add soup. Garnish with Romano cheese.

STROMBOLIOS

1 (10 oz) can refrigerated pizza dough
¼ teaspoon basil
¼ teaspoon oregano
Shaved or thinly sliced ham
Sliced black olives
Pepperoni slices
Finely shredded mozzarella cheese

Preheat oven to 400°. Lay out pizza dough on a greased foil lined baking sheet. Sprinkle with basil and oregano. Top with a thin layer of ham, black olives, pepperoni slices and mozzarella cheese. Roll up lengthwise, like a jelly roll and place seam side down. Bake about 15 minutes until golden brown. Cool slightly and cut into individual slices.

ITALIAN SAUSAGE, VEGETABLE & TORTELLINI TIMBALE

1 lb. bulk Italian sausage
6 oz. fresh baby spinach
1 (13.75 oz) can artichoke hearts, drained & sliced
4 eggs
¼ teaspoon salt
¼ teaspoon pepper
2 cups ricotta cheese
1 cup shredded Italian blend cheese
¼ cup grated Romano cheese
1 lb. fresh three cheese tortellini

Preheat oven to 375°. Cook sausage in a large skillet or saucepan over medium high heat, stirring until no longer pink. Cut spinach into chiffonade (thin strips). Add spinach and artichoke hearts to sausage and stir gently until slightly wilted. Remove from heat.

Beat eggs with a whisk in a large mixing bowl and add salt & pepper. Mix in ricotta, Italian cheese blend and Romano cheese until combined.

In the meantime, bring a large pot of salted water to a boil. Cook tortellini until tested done, about 8 minutes. Drain and stir into egg mixture. Add sausage and vegetables and mix until combined. Spoon into a greased 9 inch springform pan and cover the outside bottom of the pan with foil. Bake about 30 minutes. Cool 5 minutes before cutting into wedges. Serve with Creamy Tomato Vodka Sauce.

CREAMY TOMATO VODKA SAUCE

1 (28 oz) can crushed tomatoes
2 Tablespoons sugar
½ teaspoon salt
¼ teaspoon pepper
½ teaspoon oregano
½ teaspoon basil
2 Tablespoons Vodka
½ cup heavy cream

Place tomatoes, sugar, salt, pepper, oregano and basil in a medium saucepan over medium heat. Bring to a boil and add Vodka. Bring back to a boil and stir in cream. Heat through and serve with Timbale wedges.

CHOCOLATE BANANA ANGEL PANINI

2 (8 oz) pkgs. cream cheese, cut up
1 (13 oz) jar Nutella (chocolate hazelnut spread)
¾ cup milk
Angel Food cake
Bananas, sliced
Whipped topping
Heath chocolate toffee bits

Place cream cheese, Nutella and milk in a food processor and mix until combined and smooth.

Preheat oven to 375°. Slice angel food cake and toast slices on a greased foil lined baking sheet until lightly browned, about 5 - 10 minutes.

For each serving, spread a toasted cake slice with cream cheese mixture. Top with banana slices and sandwich with another cake slice spread with mixture. Spread top of "panini" with more cream cheese mixture and garnish with whipped topping and toffee bits.

ITALIAN CUISINE

ZUPPA DI POMODORI

GARLIC CROSTINI

LEMON CHICKEN with
OLIVES & PASTA

CHOCOLATE AMARETTO
CHEESECAKE

ZUPPA DI POMODORI

2 Tablespoons olive oil
1 small onion, finely chopped
½ cup finely chopped celery
¼ cup finely chopped carrot
1 clove garlic, pressed
4 cups beef broth, warmed
1 (10.75 oz) can tomato purée
1 teaspoon basil
Salt & pepper to taste
½ cup heavy cream
1 Tablespoon Anisette or Pernod liqueur

Heat oil in a large saucepan over medium heat. Sauté onion, celery, carrot and garlic until tender, about 10 minutes. Add beef broth, tomato purée, basil, salt and pepper. Bring to a boil, cover, lower heat and cook for 20 minutes, stirring occasionally. Add cream and Anisette. Heat thoroughly before serving. Serve with Garlic Crostini.

GARLIC CROSTINI

¼ cup butter
¼ cup olive oil
1 clove garlic, pressed
¼ teaspoon pepper
¼ cup grated Romano cheese
16 – 18 slices of Italian bread

Preheat oven to 350°. Melt butter, olive oil, garlic and pepper together. Add cheese and brush on bread slices. Bake 10 minutes.

LEMON CHICKEN WITH OLIVES & PASTA

2 Tablespoons olive oil
2 Tablespoons butter
16 - 18 chicken breast tenders
Cavender's Greek seasoning
Flour
2/3 cup dry white wine (Chardonnay)
1/3 cup lemon juice
1 clove garlic, pressed
½ cup chopped green onion
½ cup chopped parsley
1 cup olive mix (Sable & Rosenfeld Olive Bruschetta topping)

Heat olive oil and butter in a large skillet or grill pan over medium high heat. Season chicken on both sides with Cavender's. Sprinkle half the chicken with flour and cook 5 minutes on each side. Remove to a large baking dish and repeat with remaining chicken. Add wine, lemon juice, garlic, green onion, parsley and olive mix to the pan. Bring to a boil, lower heat and cook 5 minutes. Pour sauce over chicken. Can be kept warm in a low heated oven. To serve, place chicken over each serving of pasta and top with sauce.

PASTA:
1 lb. thin spaghetti, broken in half
1 Tablespoon salt
1 Tablespoon olive oil
1 cup chicken broth, warmed
½ cup grated Romano cheese
Salt & pepper to taste

Bring a large pot of water to a boil. Add 1 Tablespoon salt and stir in spaghetti. Cook until al dente (tasted done). Drain in a colander and return to pot or a bowl. Add olive oil, warm chicken broth, cheese, salt and pepper.

CHOCOLATE AMARETTO CHEESECAKE

CRUST:

18 Oreo cookies (1 ½ cups crumbs)
¼ cup toasted almond slices
¼ cup sugar
3 Tablespoons butter, cut up

Preheat oven to 375°. Place cookies and almond slices in a food processor and mix until finely crushed. Add sugar and butter and process until combined. Distribute crumb mixture evenly into the bottom and partially up the sides of a greased 9 inch springform pan. Place a piece of foil around the outside of the pan to catch any drippings. Bake for 10 minutes.

FILLING:

3 (8 oz) pkgs. cream cheese, cut up
1 cup sugar
4 eggs
1/3 cup heavy cream
¼ cup Amaretto
1 teaspoon almond extract

Beat cream cheese and sugar with an electric mixer until combined. Add eggs, one at a time. Mix in cream, Amaretto and almond extract. Mix until smooth and combined. Pour into prepared crust and bake about 45 - 50 minutes, until lightly browned and almost firm. Remove and let sit for 5 minutes.

TOPPING:

2 cups sour cream
3 Tablespoons sugar
1 teaspoon almond extract

Stir together sour cream, sugar and almond extract in a small bowl until combined. Spoon over cheesecake and spread gently to cover completely. Return to the oven and bake 5 minutes. Remove from oven and place on a rack to cool. Cover and chill completely, about 6 – 8 hours before serving. Best if made a day ahead.

GARNISH: **Toasted almond slices**

Place almond slices around the outside edge of the cheesecake and a few in a pinwheel/flower design in the center.

ITALIAN CUISINE

RAVIOLI RAVELLO

CAULIFLOWER PURÉE

CHICKEN PICCATA with CAPERS & ARTICHOKES

LIMONCELLO BLUEBERRY BREAD PUDDING

RAVIOLI RAVELLO

2 Tablespoons olive oil
1 onion, chopped
1 zucchini, quartered & sliced
2 - 3 small tomatoes, peeled & chopped
1 cup chicken broth
3 Tablespoons arugula pesto
Salt & pepper to taste
1 (9 oz.) package Four Cheese Ravioli
Grated Romano cheese

Heat oil in a saucepan over medium heat. Add onion and sauté for 5 minutes. Add zucchini, tomatoes and broth. Bring to a boil and cook 10 minutes. Stir in pesto, salt and pepper.

Bring a large pot of water to a boil, add ravioli and cook about 8 minutes. Drain and toss with sauce. Serve with cheese sprinkled on top.

CAULIFLOWER PURÉE

1 large head of cauliflower
2 Tablespoons butter, cut up
2 packets chicken broth paste (about 2 Tablespoons)
¾ cup grated Romano cheese
Salt & pepper to taste
1 teaspoon milk, if necessary

Cut cauliflower into florets. Bring a large pot of water to a boil, add cauliflower and cook about 12 minutes. Drain thoroughly. Place in a food processor and add butter, chicken broth paste, cheese, salt & pepper. Process until smooth and puréed. Taste for seasonings and add milk, only if necessary to get a smooth purée, keeping the mixture thick.

CHICKEN PICCATA with CAPERS & ARTICHOKES

16 chicken breast tenders
Salt, pepper & flour
2 Tablespoons olive oil
2 Tablespoons butter
½ cup dry white wine (Chardonnay)
1 cup chicken broth
1 (14 oz) can artichoke hearts, drained & quartered (about 10)
2 Tablespoons capers
¼ cup chopped parsley
¼ cup lemon juice
Lemon twists for garnish

Season chicken with salt, pepper and flour on both sides. Heat olive oil and butter in a large skillet over medium high heat. Add 8 tenders and cook for 5 minutes on each side. Remove, place in a large baking dish and cook second batch. Deglaze skillet with wine. Add chicken broth, artichoke hearts, capers, parsley and lemon juice. Bring to a boil until heated through (sauce will be thin). Pour sauce over chicken and serve over Cauliflower Purée with a lemon twist for garnish.

LIMONCELLO BLUEBERRY BREAD PUDDING

12 slices soft white bread
4 cups milk
¼ cup butter
3 eggs
1 ½ cups sugar
1 teaspoon lemon extract
1 cup blueberries, fresh or frozen (not thawed)

Preheat oven to 350º. Tear bread into medium size pieces and place in a large greased baking dish. Heat milk and butter in the microwave until butter melts. Pour over bread. Do not stir.

In a mixing bowl, beat eggs with a whisk and mix in sugar and lemon extract. Pour over bread and very gently push in. Sprinkle blueberries on top and very gently push in. Bake about 40 minutes until set.

SAUCE:
½ cup butter
1 cup powdered sugar
¼ cup Limoncello liqueur

Place butter and powdered sugar in a small saucepan over low heat. Stir until smooth and melted. Whisk in Limoncello and bring sauce to a boil. Serve warm bread pudding topped with warm sauce.

SOUTHWEST CUISINE

SOUTHWESTERN CALABAZA SOPA

NUEVO TAMALE TORTA with SALSA FRESCA

WARM FRUIT COBBLER MELANGE

SOUTHWESTERN CALABAZA SOPA

¼ cup butter
1 onion, chopped
2 (15 oz) cans pumpkin
4 cups chicken broth, warmed
½ teaspoon cumin
¼ teaspoon chipotle chili powder
Salt & pepper to taste
½ cup heavy cream
Cilantro or parsley leaves & extra cream for garnish

Melt butter in a large saucepan over medium heat. Add onion and sauté for 5 minutes. Stir in pumpkin, broth and seasonings. Bring to a boil and cook 10 minutes. Purée soup with an immersion blender or very carefully in a food processor. Stir in cream and heat through. Serve garnished with a leaf of cilantro or parsley and a few drops of heavy cream. NOTE: Do not use canned pumpkin pie filling!

SALSA FRESCA

1 (14.5oz) can petite diced tomatoes
1 (4oz) can diced green chilies
¼ teaspoon salt
1/8 teaspoon pepper
¼ teaspoon sugar
½ teaspoon cumin
2 Tablespoons lime juice
1 Tablespoon chopped jalapeño
Chopped cilantro, optional

Mix all ingredients together until combined. Can be made ahead and chilled. Serve with Nuevo Tamale Torta.

NUEVO TAMALE TORTA

2 lbs. ground round beef
1 onion, chopped
1 clove garlic, pressed
½ green bell pepper, chopped
2 Tablespoons chopped jalapeño
½ cup flour
¼ cup milk, warmed
1 ½ teaspoons salt
½ teaspoon pepper
2 teaspoons cumin
2 Tablespoons chili powder
2 cups shredded cheddar cheese
1 (15 oz) can pinto beans, rinsed & drained

Place ground beef in a large saucepan over medium high heat and cook, stirring occasionally, until no longer pink and most, but not all, of the liquid or fat has evaporated. Add onion, garlic, bell pepper and jalapeño and cook 5 minutes, stirring occasionally. Add flour and cook, stirring constantly, for 2 minutes. Add milk, seasonings, cheese and beans and stir until combined.

MASA CRUST:
2 ½ cups Masa Harina flour
1 teaspoon salt
1 teaspoon baking powder
1 ¼ cups chicken broth, warmed
½ cup vegetable oil

Preheat oven to 375°. Mix together masa flour, salt and baking powder in a large mixing bowl. Heat broth until warm and add oil. Stir into flour mixture until combined. Use hands to completely combine and press into the bottom and up the sides of a greased 9 inch springform pan.

Pour entire filling into the crust. Cover the outside bottom of the pan with foil, to catch any leaks. Bake for 45 minutes. Let cool 10 minutes in pan before removing sides of pan to serve.

TO SERVE:
Shredded lettuce
Salsa Fresca
Sour cream
Prepared guacamole

To serve, cut wedges of torta and surround with some shredded lettuce. Top each wedge with Salsa Fresca, sour cream and guacamole.

WARM FRUIT COBBLER MELANGE

2 red apples, peeled, cored & sliced
1 (1 lb.) bag frozen peaches
¾ cup sugar
1 Tablespoon cornstarch
½ cup dried cranberries

Preheat oven to 375°. Prepare apples and toss with peaches, sugar and cornstarch in a large bowl. Place in a greased 9 x 13 inch baking dish and top with cranberries.

TOPPING:
1 cup flour
½ cup sugar
½ teaspoon salt
½ teaspoon baking powder
1 egg, lightly beaten
½ cup butter, melted

Mix dry ingredients together and stir in egg until crumbly. Sprinkle over fruit and drizzle with melted butter. Bake for 45 minutes.

TO SERVE:
Vanilla ice cream
Toasted almond slices

Place warm cobbler in individual small bowls and top with a scoop of vanilla ice cream and garnish with almonds.

SOUTHWEST CUISINE

CORN TORTILLA SOUP

CHICKEN ENCHILADAS RANCHERO

PRALINES & CREAM DREAM

CORN TORTILLA SOUP

¼ cup vegetable oil
6 corn tortillas
1 Tablespoon vegetable oil
1 small onion, chopped
1 clove garlic, pressed
1 (8 oz) can tomato sauce
6 cups chicken broth, warmed
1 cup frozen corn
1 teaspoon cumin
2 Tablespoons lime juice
Salt & pepper to taste
Shredded Colby Jack or Fiesta blend cheese
Chopped cilantro or parsley

Heat ¼ cup oil in a large saucepan over medium heat. Cut tortillas into small strips. Fry tortilla strips in two batches, until crisp. Drain on paper towels.

Heat 1 Tablespoon oil in the same saucepan and sauté onion and garlic for 5 minutes. Add tomato sauce, broth, corn, cumin, lime juice, salt and pepper. Bring to a boil, cover and cook 15 – 20 minutes. Place some tortilla strips in each serving bowl and top with soup. Garnish with cheese and cilantro or parsley.

PRALINES & CREAM DREAM

1 cup light brown sugar
¼ cup light corn syrup
½ cup half & half cream
2 Tablespoons butter
1 cup pecan halves
½ teaspoon vanilla extract
Vanilla Ice Cream

Combine brown sugar, corn syrup and cream in a small saucepan and place over medium heat, stirring frequently to combine. Bring to a boil and cook 5 minutes, stirring occasionally. Stir in butter, pecans and vanilla, until butter melts, then remove from heat and cool before serving over vanilla ice cream. Can be stored in the refrigerator and reheated later, just until slightly warm.

CHICKEN ENCHILADAS RANCHERO

12 chicken breast tenders
Salt & pepper
1 (4.5 oz) can chopped green chiles
2 teaspoons chili powder
2 teaspoons cumin

Season chicken tenders with salt and pepper on both sides. Place in a grill pan or skillet over medium high heat and cook 5 minutes and on each side, in two batches if necessary. Remove and cut into bite size pieces. Mix with chiles, chili powder and cumin.

SAUCE:
½ cup butter
½ cup flour
2 cups chicken broth, warmed
2 cups milk, warmed
2 cups shredded cheddar cheese
¼ teaspoon salt
1/8 teaspoon pepper
1 teaspoon dry mustard
½ teaspoon Worcestershire
1 cup sour cream

Melt butter in a large saucepan over medium heat. Add flour and cook, stirring constantly for 3 minutes. Stir in heated broth and milk until combined. Cook, stirring frequently, until mixture comes to a boil. Mix in cheese and seasonings and stir until cheese melts. Remove from heat and add sour cream.

TO ASSEMBLE:
16 flour tortillas
Pepper Jack cheese, cut into small strips
Shredded lettuce
Chopped tomatoes
Guacamole

Preheat oven to 350°. Place a small amount of cheese sauce in the bottom of 2 large greased baking dishes. Fill each tortilla with chicken mixture and strips of cheese. Roll up tightly and place side by side in the baking dishes. Pour cheese sauce over enchiladas and bake, uncovered, for about 20 - 25 minutes or until hot. Garnish with lettuce, tomatoes and guacamole. If made ahead and chilled, add a little water to moisten and reheat covered with foil until hot.

SOUTHWEST CUISINE

SEDONA COLESLAW

S.W. CREAMY
MAC & CHEESE

ROASTED & GLAZED FIESTA
BBQ CHICKEN

CORONARITAS

CHOCOLATE CRUMB CAKE

SEDONA COLESLAW

16 oz bag coleslaw mix
1 cup frozen corn, thawed
1 zucchini, coarsely chopped
½ cup dried cranberries
¼ cup chopped green onion
¼ cup chopped parsley
1 (2.25 oz) can sliced black olives
½ cup crumbled feta cheese

4 corn tortillas, cut into strips & fried in 3 Tablespoons vegetable oil, until crisp

DRESSING:
½ cup olive oil
3 Tablespoons lime juice
½ teaspoon salt
¼ teaspoon pepper
½ teaspoon cumin
1 teaspoon sugar
¼ teaspoon Dijon mustard

Place slaw, corn, zucchini, cranberries, green onion, parsley, black olives and feta in a large bowl and toss. Prepare tortilla strips to use as garnish. Whisk together dressing ingredients and toss with coleslaw mixture. Garnish each serving with broken tortilla strips.

S.W. CREAMY MAC & CHEESE

2 Tablespoons butter
2 Tablespoons flour
1 ½ cups milk, warmed
1 teaspoon salt
½ teaspoon pepper
½ teaspoon dry mustard
1 (4.5 oz) can chopped green chilies
2 cups shredded cheddar cheese
2 oz. Pepper Jack cheese, cut up

1 Tablespoon salt
16 oz. elbow macaroni

Melt butter in a large saucepan over medium heat. Stir in flour and cook, stirring constantly, for 2 minutes. Add warmed milk, seasonings and cheeses. Stir until melted and heated through. Bring a large pot of water to a boil, add salt and cook macaroni until tested done. Drain and toss with sauce. Add extra milk when reheating.

ROASTED & GLAZED FIESTA BBQ CHICKEN

DRY RUB:
1 Tablespoon salt
1 Tablespoon pepper
1 Tablespoon brown sugar
1 Tablespoon dry mustard
1 Tablespoon chili powder

24 boneless, skinless chicken thighs (about 6 lbs)

GLAZE:
2 cups Dr. Pepper
1 cup ketchup
2 Tablespoons cider vinegar
¼ cup brown sugar
½ teaspoon salt
¼ teaspoon pepper
2 Tablespoons Hot Squeeze chipotle sauce

Preheat oven to 375º. Mix together all ingredients for dry rub in a small bowl. Trim any excess fat from chicken thighs and place in a large greased foil lined baking pan. Sprinkle half of seasoning mixture on chicken and lightly rub in. Turn chicken over and repeat. Place chicken in the oven and roast for 50 minutes.

Meanwhile, place all ingredients for glaze in a medium size saucepan and whisk over medium heat. Bring to a boil, lower heat as necessary, but maintain a boil. Cook for 30 minutes. Brush glaze over one side of the chicken and return to the oven for about 15 minutes. (Baby Back Ribs can be substituted for chicken thighs. Increase roasting time by 10 minutes.)

CORONARITAS

1 (12 oz) can frozen limeade concentrate
1 (12 oz) bottle chilled Sprite
1 (12 oz) bottle chilled Corona beer
4 oz. or more Tequila

Mix together all ingredients in a pitcher and serve over ice. (Makes 40 oz)

CHOCOLATE CRUMB CAKE

TOPPING:
½ cup pecans, chopped
1 cup graham cracker crumbs (9 whole crackers)
¼ cup butter, melted
½ cup semisweet chocolate chips

CAKE:
1 cup butter
½ cup cocoa
2 cups sugar
2 eggs
1 cup buttermilk
1 teaspoon vanilla
1 teaspoon baking soda
2 cups flour

Preheat oven to 375º. Chop pecans in a food processor by pulsing lightly. Remove to a small bowl. Add graham crackers to food processor and mix until finely crushed. Add to pecans with melted butter and chocolate chips. Stir together until combined.

Place butter and cocoa in a medium saucepan over medium heat. Heat until butter melts and cocoa dissolves. Remove from heat and whisk in sugar. Whisk in eggs, buttermilk, vanilla and baking soda. Add flour and stir until combined. Pour into a greased 9 x 13 inch baking pan and sprinkle topping over cake batter. Bake about 35 – 40 minutes, until tested done. Let cool in pan.

TO SERVE:
Dulce de Leche sauce, warmed
Whipped cream

Cut squares of cake and top with a drizzle of sauce and a dollop of whipped cream.

SPRINGTIME CELEBRATION

SPINACH SALAD with BERRIES & PECANS

CAJUN PEPPERED SHRIMP & GRITS

LEMON CELEBRATION CAKE

SPINACH SALAD with BERRIES & PECANS

¼ cup Vanilla Fig Balsamic vinegar
¾ cup olive oil
1 teaspoon sugar
½ teaspoon salt
¼ teaspoon pepper
1 teaspoon Dijon mustard

Fresh baby spinach
Strawberries
Blueberries
Crumbled feta cheese
Toasted pecans

Whisk together vinegar, olive oil, sugar, salt, pepper and Dijon mustard for the salad dressing. Can be made ahead and chilled.

Make individual salads by placing spinach on each plate. Wash, hull and slice strawberries. Top spinach with strawberries, blueberries, feta cheese and toasted pecans. Drizzle with dressing.

CAJUN PEPPERED SHRIMP & GRITS

GRITS:

2 cups water
2 cups chicken broth
2 cups milk
2 teaspoons salt
1 ½ cups Quick Grits
2 Tablespoons butter
2 cups shredded cheddar cheese
2 oz. Pepper Jack cheese, cut up

Place water, broth and milk in a large saucepan over medium high heat and bring to a boil. Stir constantly while adding salt and grits. Lower heat to medium, cover loosely and cook until grits thicken, stirring occasionally to keep from sticking. Turn heat down to low. Add butter and cheeses and cook until cheese melts.

SHRIMP:

½ cup butter
¼ cup olive oil
3 lbs. medium shrimp, peeled
1 clove garlic, pressed
1 cup chopped green onion
1 cup sliced mushrooms
½ cup chopped parsley
½ teaspoon salt
1 teaspoon pepper
¼ teaspoon cayenne pepper
½ teaspoon paprika
¼ teaspoon basil, thyme & oregano
1 Tablespoon lemon juice
Hot French bread

In a large saucepan, melt butter and oil over medium high heat. Add shrimp and sauté just until pink. Stir in all other ingredients and seasonings. Lower heat, cover and cook 10 minutes. Mixture will be very saucy. Serve a spoonful of grits surrounded with shrimp and sauce in shallow bowls. Serve with hot French bread for dipping.

LEMON CELEBRATION CAKE

1 cup butter, softened
2 cups sugar
3 eggs
Zest of 1 lemon
2 teaspoons baking powder
½ teaspoon salt
2 cups flour
1 cup sour cream

Preheat oven to 350º. In a large bowl, cream butter and sugar with an electric mixer until fluffy, about 4 minutes. Add eggs, one at a time, until mixed. Add lemon zest, baking powder and salt. Mix in flour alternately with sour cream until blended.

Pour into a greased bundt pan and bake about 50 minutes or until tested done. Let cool in pan for 10 minutes. Remove and place on a wire rack to cool completely before glazing.

GLAZE:

2 cups powdered sugar
3 Tablespoons fresh lemon juice
1 drop yellow food coloring
Decorative sprinkles

Mix powdered sugar, lemon juice and food coloring in a small bowl to obtain a smooth consistency. Spoon glaze all over cake and top with decorative sprinkles.

SPRINGTIME CELEBRATION

SPRING SALAD of APPLES, GORGONZOLA & PECANS with POMEGRANATE VINAIGRETTE

SMASHED POTATOES

SAUTÉED FISH with ROASTED RED PEPPERS & CREOLE MUSTARD SAUCE

"BEST OF THE BEST" AMARETTO BREAD PUDDING

SPRING SALAD of APPLES, GORGONZOLA & PECANS with POMEGRANATE VINAIGRETTE

2 cups Cran-Pomegranate Juice
½ cup olive oil
¼ teaspoon sugar
½ teaspoon salt
¼ teaspoon pepper
¼ teaspoon Dijon mustard
¾ cup pecans, broken in half
2 Tablespoons Hot Squeeze
Butter lettuce
Green apple, sliced thin
Crumbled Gorgonzola cheese

Bring Cran-Pomegranate juice to a boil in a small saucepan over high heat and reduce to ½ cup, about 12 - 15 minutes. Cool about 15 minutes. Whisk in olive oil, sugar, salt, pepper and mustard. Chill.

Toast pecans in a skillet over medium heat and toss with Hot Squeeze Chipotle Sauce. Let cool and separate. Prepare individual salads of butter lettuce, apple slices, Gorgonzola cheese and pecans. Drizzle with dressing.

SMASHED POTATOES

1 ½ lbs. small white or red potatoes
Salt & pepper to taste
¼ cup butter, melted
½ cup chicken broth
Sweet Onion cane sugar by FlavorStorm

Scrub potatoes clean but do not peel. Bring about 8 cups of water to a boil in a large stockpot over high heat. Cut potatoes in half or quarters, depending on size, and add to boiling water. Cook about 15 minutes, until tender. Drain and place in a baking dish. Mash down once with a potato masher to smash the potatoes. Sprinkle all over with salt and pepper. Drizzle with butter and broth and sprinkle generously with Sweet Onion sugar. Place in a low heated oven to keep warm.

SAUTÉED FISH with ROASTED RED PEPPERS & CREOLE MUSTARD SAUCE

8 catfish fillets
Salt, pepper & flour
2 Tablespoons butter
2 Tablespoons vegetable oil
½ cup chopped green onion
¼ cup chopped roasted red peppers
½ cup dry white wine (Chardonnay)
¼ cup heavy cream
3 Tablespoons Creole mustard

Season fish with salt and pepper on both sides. Heat butter and oil in a large skillet over medium high heat. Flour one side of 4 fillets and place flour side down in skillet. Cook 5 minutes, flour and flip. Cook 5 minutes more. Place in a baking dish and keep warm in a low heated oven. Repeat cooking the remaining fish in the same skillet, 5 minutes on each side and remove fish to the baking dish. Stir green onion and peppers into remaining oil in the skillet. Add wine to deglaze the pan and cook 1 minute. Stir in cream and mustard until blended and heated through. Pour sauce over fillets and serve immediately or keep warm in the oven.

"BEST OF THE BEST" AMARETTO BREAD PUDDING

12 slices of soft white bread
4 cups milk
¼ cup butter
3 eggs
1 ½ cups sugar
1 teaspoon almond extract

SAUCE:
½ cup butter
1 cup powdered sugar
¼ cup Amaretto

Preheat oven to 350º. Tear up bread into medium size pieces and place in a large greased baking dish. Heat milk and butter in the microwave until butter melts. Pour over bread. In a mixing bowl, beat eggs with a whisk and mix in sugar and almond extract. Pour over bread and gently stir in. Bake about 40 minutes until set.

Make sauce by melting butter and powdered sugar in a small saucepan over low heat, stirring until smooth. Whisk in Amaretto until smooth and sauce comes to a boil. Serve warm bread pudding topped with warm sauce. (Can be made ahead and reheated in the microwave).

SUMMER CUISINE

SAVORY VEGETABLE FRITTATA

MEDITERRANEAN BREAD

ATHENIAN GRILLED CHICKEN COBB SALAD

WHITE CHOCOLATE PANNA COTTA with SWEET LEMON SAUCE

SAVORY VEGETABLE FRITTATA

6 eggs
¼ cup half & half cream
½ teaspoon salt
¼ teaspoon pepper
1/8 teaspoon cayenne
½ cup roasted red peppers, coarsely chopped
1 cup sliced mushrooms
¼ cup chopped green onion
¼ cup chopped parsley
½ cup shredded Asiago cheese
Prepared Basil Pesto for garnish

Preheat oven to 350°. Beat eggs with a whisk to combine. Add cream, salt, pepper and cayenne. Grease a 9 – 10 inch quiche dish or pie pan with cooking spray. Place roasted peppers, mushrooms, green onion, parsley and cheese in the dish. Pour egg mixture over vegetables and bake for about 20 - 25 minutes. Serve warm with a garnish of Pesto.

MEDITERRANEAN BREAD

1 loaf French bread
½ cup butter, softened
¼ cup olive oil
1 clove garlic, pressed
¼ cup grated Romano or Parmesan cheese
¼ teaspoon pepper

Preheat oven to 350°. Slice French bread into individual slices and reassemble, to form a loaf shape. Place on a greased foil lined baking pan. Mix together butter, olive oil, garlic, cheese and pepper. Spread completely over bread and bake for about 8 minutes.

ATHENIAN GRILLED CHICKEN COBB SALAD

GRILLED CHICKEN:
16 chicken breast tenders
¼ cup lemon juice
¼ cup olive oil
1 clove garlic, pressed
½ teaspoon salt
¼ teaspoon pepper
¼ teaspoon oregano
1 teaspoon cayenne pepper
1 Tablespoon Dijon mustard
Cavender's Greek Seasoning

DRESSING:
1 cup olive oil
1/3 cup Vanilla Fig Balsamic Vinegar
½ teaspoon salt
¼ teaspoon pepper
1 cup crumbled feta cheese

SALAD:
Mixed leaf lettuce & fresh spinach
Shredded carrots
Sliced black olives
Avocado, cut up
Cucumber, sliced
Grape tomatoes, chopped
Boiled eggs, chopped

Place chicken tenders in a large Ziploc bag. Mix together lemon juice, olive oil, garlic, salt, pepper, oregano, cayenne and Dijon mustard with a whisk until combined. Pour over chicken and let marinate 15 – 30 minutes.

Place a large stovetop grill pan or skillet over medium high heat and cook chicken 5 minutes on one side. Before turning chicken over, sprinkle each piece with Cavender's Greek Seasoning. Turn and cook another 5 minutes. Let cool slightly and cut into bite size pieces.

Make dressing by combining all ingredients with a whisk. Cover and chill.

Assemble salads by placing a mixture of leaf lettuce and spinach on each individual plate. Top with shredded carrots. Add chicken pieces, black olives, avocado, cucumber, tomatoes and boiled eggs, in order. Drizzle with dressing before serving. (Serves 8)

WHITE CHOCOLATE PANNA COTTA

2 pkgs. unflavored gelatin
¼ cup water
1 ½ cups heavy cream
½ cup powdered sugar
4 oz. white chocolate, chopped
1 ½ cups buttermilk
Strawberry or mint for garnish

Stir gelatin into water and let stand. Place heavy cream and powdered sugar in a 4 cup glass measurer and whisk to combine. Microwave until boiling, about 2 minutes. Whisk in chopped white chocolate until melted. Add gelatin and stir to dissolve. Add buttermilk and whisk until smooth. Pour into eight (4 oz) greased custard cups or molds. Chill until firm, about 1 hour. Unmold to serve with Sweet Lemon Sauce and garnish with a fresh strawberry or mint, if desired.

SWEET LEMON SAUCE

½ cup sugar
2 Tablespoons cornstarch
1 cup water
3 Tablespoons butter
Zest of 1 lemon
2 Tablespoons lemon juice

Combine sugar, cornstarch and water in a small saucepan and whisk together. Place over medium heat and bring to a boil, stirring frequently. Remove and add butter, lemon zest and lemon juice. Cool before using. Store in the refrigerator.

SUMMER CUISINE

SOUTH OF THE BORDER BEAN DIP

BAJA GRILLED FISH TACOS

CORONARITAS

BALSAMIC STRAWBERRIES & ICE CREAM DREAM

SOUTH OF THE BORDER BEAN DIP

2 (15 oz) cans pinto beans
½ teaspoon salt
½ teaspoon chipotle chili powder
1 teaspoon cumin
1 teaspoon chili powder
½ cup crumbled cooked bacon
½ cup sour cream
½ cup shredded cheddar cheese
½ cup chopped grape tomatoes

2 (15 oz) cans black beans
½ teaspoon salt
1/8 teaspoon chipotle chili powder
1 teaspoon cumin
¼ cup prepared tomato salsa
½ cup prepared tomato salsa
½ cup shredded Fiesta cheese
1 (4 oz) can chopped green chilies
Shredded lettuce for garnish

Place pinto beans in a colander, drain and rinse with cold water. Place in a food processor and add salt, chipotle chili powder, cumin and chili powder. Mix until combined and smooth. Spread dip on one side of a large platter. Top with a layer of bacon, sour cream, cheddar cheese and tomatoes.

Place black beans in a colander, drain and rinse with cold water. Place in a food processor and add salt, chipotle chili powder, cumin and ¼ cup salsa. Mix until combined and smooth. Spread black bean dip on the other side of the pinto bean dip. Top with a layer of ½ cup salsa, cheese and green chilies. Garnish with shredded lettuce around the edge of the platter. Serve with tortilla chips.

BAJA GRILLED FISH TACOS

8 fish fillets (any whitefish such as catfish, tilapia, mahi mahi, halibut, etc.)
Lemon pepper seasoning
Hot Squeeze Sweet Chipotle Sauce
8 Fajita size flour tortillas, warmed
Coleslaw mix
Prepared guacamole

BAJA CREAM:
1 cup sour cream
Zest of 1 lime
¼ cup lime juice
½ teaspoon salt
½ teaspoon pepper

Season fish fillets with a light sprinkling of Lemon Pepper on both sides of fish. Heat a grill pan greased with cooking spray over medium high heat. Cook fillets about 5 minutes on each side. (According to the size of the fillets, cook 10 minutes per inch of thickness.) Brush with a light layer of sweet chipotle sauce. Can keep warm in a low heated oven.

In the meantime, prepare Baja Cream by stirring together all ingredients until combined.

To serve, place a fish fillet in a warm tortilla. Top with some coleslaw mix, Baja Cream and guacamole. (Makes 8 fish tacos)

CORONARITAS

1 (12 oz) can frozen limeade concentrate
1 (12 oz) bottle chilled Sprite
1 (12 oz bottle chilled Corona beer
4 oz (or more) Tequila

Combine all ingredients in a pitcher, stir until combined. Serve over ice. (Makes 40 oz)

BALSAMIC STRAWBERRIES & ICE CREAM DREAM

Fresh strawberries
Sugar
Vanilla Fig Balsamic Vinegar
Hershey's chocolate syrup
Blue Bell Strawberries & Homemade Vanilla Ice Cream

Wash, hull and slice strawberries. Sprinkle with sugar. Let sit in the refrigerator for about 30 minutes to form a syrup. Stir occasionally. Drizzle with Balsamic vinegar before serving.

Drizzle ice cream bowls with some chocolate syrup. Add a couple of scoops of ice cream and top with Balsamic strawberries. (Make any amount desired)

SUMMER CUISINE

MEDITERRANEAN HUMMUS with PITA CRISPS

STACKED SUMMER SALAD with RUSSIAN DRESSING

ITALIAN ZUCCHINI FRITTATA

BOSTON ICE CREAM PIE

MEDITERRANEAN HUMMUS

1 (15 oz) can chick peas (garbanzo beans)
1 clove garlic, pressed
¼ cup lemon juice
1 Tablespoon olive oil
¼ cup tahini (sesame seed paste)
½ teaspoon salt
¼ teaspoon pepper
½ teaspoon cumin
¼ teaspoon cayenne pepper
Paprika & parsley for garnish

Drain and rinse chick peas. Mix all ingredients in a food processor until smooth and combined. Add a little water if too thick. Garnish with paprika & parsley.

PITA CRISPS

4 pita breads
¼ cup butter, melted

Preheat oven to 425°. Cut each pita bread in half, then into 8 triangles. Separate top from bottom. Place on a large greased foil lined baking sheet. Brush each piece with melted butter and toast for about 6 – 8 minutes, until golden brown.

STACKED SUMMER SALAD

RUSSIAN DRESSING:

1 ½ cups mayonnaise
¾ cup ketchup
2 Tablespoons lemon juice
2 Tablespoons Hot Squeeze Sweet Chipotle Sauce
2 Tablespoons dill pickle relish

Stir together all ingredients for dressing and chill.

SALAD:

Butter lettuce, chopped
Broccoli florets, chopped
Thin sliced ham, chopped
Tomatoes, chopped
Mushrooms, chopped
Shredded carrots
Crumbled cooked bacon

Spray the inside of an empty tin can (3 inches round x 3 inches tall), with top and bottom removed, with Pam. Place on an individual serving dish or shallow bowl. Toss together lettuce and broccoli with enough dressing to moisten. Place a layer of lettuce & broccoli in the bottom and use a tart tamper to press down each of the following layers on top: ham, tomatoes, mushrooms, another layer of lettuce & broccoli, then carrots. Carefully remove can, drizzle with a little dressing and garnish with bacon.

ITALIAN ZUCCHINI FRITTATA

2 Tablespoons olive oil
½ onion, chopped
1 clove garlic, pressed
½ lb. zucchini (2 small)
¼ teaspoon Cavender's
10 eggs
1 teaspoon salt
¼ teaspoon pepper
1 teaspoon basil
2 Tablespoons Italian breadcrumbs
¼ cup grated Romano cheese
1 cup shredded cheddar cheese
1 large tomato, sliced

Preheat oven to 350°. Heat oil in a large skillet over medium heat. Sauté onion and garlic about 5 minutes. Meanwhile, shred zucchini in a food processor and add to onion mixture. Cook 2 minutes. Add Cavender's and let cool slightly.

Beat eggs with a whisk in a large mixing bowl. Add salt, pepper, basil and breadcrumbs. Stir in onion mixture. Pour into a greased 9 or 10 inch quiche dish or pie pan. Sprinkle with cheeses and arrange tomato slices on top.

Bake about 25 minutes, until set. Let cool slightly before serving.

BOSTON ICE CREAM PIE

ICE CREAM:
1qt. (4 cups) vanilla ice cream

Soften ice cream and spread into a greased foil lined 9 inch cake pan. Cover and freeze until firm.

CAKE:
2 eggs
½ cup sour cream
1 cup sugar
1 teaspoon vanilla
¼ teaspoon salt
1 teaspoon baking powder
¼ teaspoon baking soda
1 cup flour

Preheat oven to 350°. With an electric mixer, beat eggs and sour cream for 2 minutes. Add sugar and beat 2 minutes more. Add vanilla, then mix in dry ingredients until blended. Pour batter into a greased 9 inch round cake pan and bake about 20 – 25 minutes, until tested done. Cool in pan 10 minutes. Turn out on a rack to cool completely. Make glaze and icing.

CHOCOLATE GLAZE:
1 oz. unsweetened chocolate
1 Tablespoon butter
1 cup powdered sugar
½ teaspoon vanilla
About 2 Tablespoons water

Carefully melt chocolate and butter in the microwave on half power. Stir to check melting. Mix with powdered sugar, vanilla and just enough water to obtain a spreading consistency.

VANILLA ICING:
½ cup powdered sugar
About 1 Tablespoon water

Combine powdered sugar and enough water to obtain a drizzling consistency. Place in a small Ziploc bag.

(Continued on next page)

(Boston Ice Cream Pie continued)

TO ASSEMBLE:

When cake is cool, mark with toothpicks as a guide and cut cake horizontally into 2 layers, using a long serrated knife. Mark the top layer with a toothpick and just underneath it mark the bottom layer. Place bottom layer on a plate and unmold ice cream on top. Place top cake layer on ice cream, lining up toothpicks, and spread chocolate glaze over top of cake and to drip a little over the sides. Snip off a tiny corner of the Ziploc and drizzle vanilla icing in a spiral pattern starting from the center. Before icing has set, draw the dull edge of a knife though the icing, starting from the center at regular intervals, to produce a spider web effect. Freeze.

SUMMER CUISINE

HOT & SPICY DEVILED EGGS

HALF & HALF COOLERS

ATHENIAN CHICKEN & ORZO SALADE with ROASTED GARLIC VINAIGRETTE

CANDY BAR BROWNIE MUFFINS

HOT & SPICY DEVILED EGGS

12 eggs
¼ cup sour cream
¼ cup mayonnaise
¼ teaspoon salt
3 Tablespoons or more Pepper Jelly
Zest of a lime & black pepper

Place eggs in a large saucepan and cover with about an inch of water. Place on high heat, start timer for 20 minutes and let boil. Remove from heat, drain and cover with cold water. Peel eggs and cut in half. Remove yolks and place in a small bowl. Mash yolks with sour cream, mayonnaise, salt and pepper jelly. Taste for seasoning. Use a small ice cream scoop to place yolk mixture into egg white halves. Garnish with a tiny zest of lime and a sprinkling of pepper.

HALF & HALF COOLERS

Lemonade, chilled
Brewed tea, chilled

Pour Lemonade into a small glass about half way up. Gently pour tea over a spoon placed at an angle held over the lemonade, to keep the halves separated.

ATHENIAN CHICKEN & ORZO SALADE with ROASTED GARLIC VINAIGRETTE

ROASTED GARLIC VINAIGRETTE:

2 heads (bulbs) garlic
½ teaspoon olive oil

Preheat oven to 325°. Cut a small slice off the top of the whole garlic heads to expose garlic cloves. Place in a garlic roaster, small baking dish or aluminum foil, drizzle with olive oil, cover and roast for 30 minutes. Remove cover and roast 30 minutes more. When cool enough to handle, squeeze garlic pulp from peel.

1 cup olive oil
¼ cup balsamic vinegar
1 ½ teaspoons salt
1 teaspoon pepper
1 teaspoon Dijon mustard

Place oil, vinegar, salt, pepper and mustard in a food processor. Add roasted garlic and mix until combined.

ORZO:

1 lb. orzo pasta
1 cup frozen corn, thawed
1 zucchini, coarsely chopped
1 yellow squash, coarsely chopped
¼ cup chopped roasted red bell pepper
¼ cup chopped green onion
¼ cup chopped parsley
½ cup crumbled feta cheese
¼ cup grated Romano cheese

Bring a large pot of salted water to a boil. Add orzo pasta and cook for about 10 minutes, until tasted done. Drain thoroughly and place in a large bowl. Add all remaining ingredients and toss together with Roasted Garlic Vinaigrette.

(Continued on next page)

(Athenian Chicken & Orzo Salade continued)

CHICKEN:

16 chicken breast tenders
Cavender's Greek seasoning
3 Tablespoons Russian Sweet & Hot Mustard, warmed

Season chicken on both sides with Cavender's. Heat a large grill pan, sprayed with Pam, over medium high heat and cook 8 chicken tenders for 5 minutes on each side. Remove from pan and brush with mustard. Repeat with remaining chicken tenders.

TO SERVE:

Sliced black olives
Crumbled feta cheese
Dried cranberries
Shelled sunflower seeds
Grape tomatoes, halved
Cucumber, sliced

To serve, place Orzo Salade on a large platter. Top with olives, feta cheese, cranberries and sunflower seeds. Place chicken tenders on top of salade and garnish edges of platter with tomatoes and cucumbers.

CANDY BAR BROWNIE MUFFINS

¾ cup butter
4 oz. unsweetened chocolate
1½ cups sugar
3 eggs
¼ teaspoon salt
1 teaspoon vanilla
1 cup flour
24 mini Snickers candies, cut in half diagonally

Preheat oven to 350°. Place butter and chocolate in the microwave and heat on half power until butter melts. Whisk until chocolate melts. Mix in sugar, then whisk in eggs, salt and vanilla. Add flour and stir to combine.

Line a 12 cup muffin tin with paper liners and spray the inside of the papers heavily with cooking spray. Place a half a scoop of batter in each cup, top with 2 pieces of cut candy, cut side down, on top. Add another half scoop of batter and finish with 2 pieces of cut candy on top. Bake about 20 minutes. Let cool in pan.

SUMMER CUISINE

BLT AVOCADO SOUP

MEDITERRANEAN TOMATO & CUCUMBER SALAD

SOUTHWESTERN CHICKEN WRAPS

TOASTED ALMOND ANGEL CAKE with FRESH BERRIES

BLT AVOCADO SOUP

1 avocado, peeled & cut
¾ - 1 cup chicken broth
½ cup sour cream
1 Tablespoon lemon juice
1/8 teaspoon salt
2 Tablespoons Hot Squeeze
Garnish: cooked, crumbled bacon and grape tomato slivers

Place avocado, broth, sour cream, lemon juice, salt and Hot Squeeze in a food processor and mix until combined. Serve in small glasses garnished with a tiny sprinkle of bacon and a sliver of tomato. Add more broth if too thick.

MEDITERRANEAN TOMATO & CUCUMBER SALAD with GRILLED BREAD

Tomatoes, cut into wedges
Cucumber, peeled & sliced
Black olives
Capers
Salt or Cavender's Greek Seasoning
Fresh ground pepper
Grated Romano cheese
Balsamic vinegar
Extra Virgin olive oil
Feta cheese, sliced or crumbled
Fresh basil chiffonade

GRILLED BREAD:
Crusty French bread, sliced
Extra Virgin olive oil

For each salad, place some tomato, cucumber, black olives and capers in individual bowls. Sprinkle with salt, pepper and Romano cheese. Drizzle with vinegar and olive oil. Top with a slice of Feta cheese and garnish with basil.

GRILLED BREAD: Heat a large grill pan or skillet over medium high heat. Add slices of bread and toast on each side. Drizzle one side with olive oil.

SOUTHWESTERN CHICKEN WRAPS

DRESSING:
1 ½ cups sour cream
¼ cup fresh lime juice
1 teaspoon salt
½ teaspoon pepper
½ teaspoon paprika
1 teaspoon cumin
½ cup chopped green onion
¼ cup chopped parsley

WRAPS:
16 chicken breast tenders
Salt & pepper
Hot Squeeze Chipotle Sauce
Burrito size tortillas
1 can black beans, rinsed
2 cups frozen corn, thawed
Tomatoes, chopped
Prepared guacamole
Baby spinach, chopped

Mix dressing ingredients in a small bowl until combined. Season chicken with salt and pepper. Heat a large skillet, sprayed with Pam, over medium high heat and cook chicken, in two batches, for 5 minutes on each side. Remove and brush Hot Squeeze on both sides of chicken. Cut into chunks and mix with dressing.

To make individual wraps, place in order on burrito size tortillas: chicken mixture, black beans, corn, tomato, guacamole and spinach. Fold ends in and roll up to enclose filling. Cut in half at a diagonal.

TOASTED ALMOND ANGEL CAKE with FRESH BERRIES

1 pint fresh strawberries
¼ cup sugar
1 cup fresh blueberries
Prepared angel food cake
2 eggs
¼ cup milk
¼ cup Amaretto
Whipped cream
Toasted almond slices

Rinse and hull strawberries. Slice and place in a bowl with sugar. Stir until juicy. Rinse blueberries.

Cut 8 slices of angel food cake. In a shallow bowl, whisk together eggs, milk and Amaretto. Dip cake slices in eggs mixture to coat both sides. Place 1 batch in a large skillet, sprayed with Pam, over medium heat. Cook slices about 5 minutes on each side until lightly browned.

Serve cake topped with strawberries, blueberries, whipped cream and almond slices.

YOUNG EVERYDAY GOURMET

PEPPY PIZZA QUESADILLAS

PACO TACOS with QUESO SAUCE

COCO LOCO CUPCAKES

PACO TACOS

1 ½ lbs. ground round beef
2 Tablespoons chili powder
1 Tablespoon cumin
2 Tablespoons Hidden Valley Ranch salad dressing mix
2 Tablespoons water
8 (1 oz) bags of Fritoes

Place ground beef in a large greased skillet and cook over medium high heat until no longer pink, stirring frequently and breaking meat up into small pieces. Add chili powder, cumin, Hidden Valley Ranch Mix and water. Stir until combined. Keep warm over very low heat while making Queso Sauce.

To serve tacos, gently crush Fritoes in each bag. Open bags and top with seasoned ground beef. Spoon Queso Sauce on top and serve. Eat right out of the bag!

QUESO SAUCE

2 Tablespoons butter
1 Tablespoon cornstarch
1 ½ cups sour cream
2 cups finely shredded cheddar or Colby Jack cheese
¼ cup prepared salsa

Melt butter in a small saucepan over medium heat. Mix cornstarch into sour cream and stir into butter. Cook until bubbly. Stir in cheese and salsa. Cook until sauce is smooth and saucy, about 10 minutes, stirring occasionally.

PEPPY PIZZA QUESADILLAS

Fajita size flour tortillas
Prepared salsa
Pepperoni slices
Shredded mozzarella cheese
Grated Romano cheese

Preheat oven to 350°. Spread one half of each tortilla with about 1 teaspoon salsa. Top with 2 slices of pepperoni, cut into fourths. Add 3 Tablespoons shredded mozzarella cheese and 1 Tablespoon Romano cheese. Fold tortilla in half. Cut tortilla in half and place a toothpick, at an angle, in each half to hold together. Place Quesadillas on a greased foil lined baking pan and bake for 5 minutes. Make as many as you like!

COCO LOCO CUPCAKES

½ cup butter
½ cup cocoa
1 ½ cups sugar
2 eggs
1 ½ cups milk
1 teaspoon vanilla
½ teaspoon salt
2 teaspoons baking powder
1 2/3 cups flour
Heath Toffee Bits

Preheat oven to 350°. Place butter in a large microwave proof bowl and microwave for about 1 minute, until melted. Whisk in cocoa and sugar until combined. Add 2 eggs, milk and vanilla. Add salt, baking powder and flour and stir until combined. Spoon about 1 Tablespoon batter into mini muffin tins greased with cooking spray. Top batter with ½ teaspoon Heath Toffee Bits and then top with another 1 Tablespoon batter. Bake 10 minutes, until tested done. Let cool in pans. (Makes about 60 mini muffins)

ICING:
¼ cup butter
3 Tablespoons cocoa
2 Tablespoons milk
1 teaspoon vanilla
2 cups powdered sugar
White sparkling sugar sprinkles

Place butter in a microwave proof bowl and microwave for about 30 seconds, until melted. Whisk in cocoa, milk, vanilla and powdered sugar until combined and smooth. Spread a small amount of icing on each cooled cupcake and sprinkle with sugar sprinkles.

YOUNG EVERYDAY GOURMET

CHICKEN, HAM & CHEESE MEAT PIES

SAUCY SUGARED CARROTS

RAINBOW FRUIT SLUSHY

CRISPY PEANUT BUTTER TOFFEE BITES

CHICKEN, HAM & CHEESE MEAT PIES

4 chicken breast tenders
Salt & pepper to taste
2 Tablespoons butter
¼ cup flour
½ cup chicken broth, warmed
¼ teaspoon poultry seasoning
¼ teaspoon salt
¼ teaspoon pepper
1 cup shredded cheddar cheese
½ cup chopped ham
1 (15 oz) box refrigerated pie crust dough (2 crusts)

Sprinkle chicken tenders with salt and pepper on both sides. Heat a small skillet sprayed with cooking spray over medium high heat. Add chicken and cook 5 minutes. Turn pieces over and cook 5 minutes more. Remove and let cool.

In a small saucepan, melt butter over medium heat. Add flour and stir constantly for 2 minutes. Add warm chicken broth and stir to combine. Mix in poultry seasoning, salt, pepper, cheese and ham. Mixture will be very thick.

Shred chicken pieces with 2 forks and add to filling. Let cool.

Preheat oven to 400°. Lay out pie crust dough and cut circles out, very close together, with a 3 inch round cookie/biscuit cutter. Use a pastry brush or fingers to moisten the edges of the circles with a little water. Place 1 Tablespoon filling in the circle. Fold dough over filling to make a half moon or crescent shape. Press edges together with a fork to crimp and seal. Roll any extra dough out and cut out more circles until all the dough is used.

Place meat pies on 2 greased foil lined baking sheets and bake 12 – 14 minutes, until lightly browned. Makes about 24 small meat pies.

SAUCY SUGARED CARROTS

1 lb. baby carrots
2 Tablespoons butter
¼ cup sugar
¼ cup light brown sugar
¼ cup prepared orange juice
½ teaspoon cinnamon
1 teaspoon vanilla

Place 4 cups of water in a medium size saucepan and bring to a boil over high heat. Add carrots and cook for 10 minutes. Drain water from carrots in a colander. Place carrots back in saucepan and add butter, sugar, brown sugar, orange juice, cinnamon and vanilla. Return to stove, lower heat to medium and cook 5 minutes more.

RAINBOW FRUIT SLUSHY

½ cup Strawberry flavored soda (Fanta), chilled
½ cup Orange flavored soda, chilled
½ cup Grape flavored soda, chilled

Measure chilled ingredients in a 16 oz. plastic cup for each serving. Place in the freezer for 1 – 2 hours, until slushy. Serve with a straw.

CRISPY PEANUT BUTTER TOFFEE BITES

¼ cup butter
1 cup creamy peanut butter
2 cups Rice Krispies cereal
½ cup Heath Toffee Bits
2 – 2 ½ cups powdered sugar
Powdered sugar for garnish

Place butter in a large microwave proof bowl. Melt butter in the microwave for about 30 seconds. Stir in peanut butter until smooth. Mix in Rice Krispies, toffee bits and powdered sugar until combined. Mixture will be stiff and a little dry. Mix together with hands, if necessary, and add more powdered sugar if too moist.

Pinch off about 1 Tablespoon size portions and roll into balls in your hands. Spray hands with cooking spray to keep mixture from sticking to hands. Garnish with a sprinkle of powdered sugar. Can be chilled. Makes about 3 dozen bites.

YOUNG EVERYDAY GOURMET

MEXICAN SPAGHETTI

SESAME CORN BISCUITS

STRAWBERRY ANGEL CAKE

MEXICAN SPAGHETTI

1 ½ lbs. ground round beef
1 (16 oz) jar "On the Border" mild salsa
1 (29 oz) can "Hunt's" tomato sauce
2 teaspoons cumin
2 Tablespoons chili powder
Salt & pepper to taste
2 cups frozen corn
1 lb. pkg. thin spaghetti
1 cup shredded cheddar cheese

Grease a large pot with cooking spray and place over medium high heat. Add ground beef and cook, stirring frequently, until no longer pink. Stir in salsa, tomato sauce, cumin, chili powder, salt, pepper and corn. Cook until mixture begins to boil. Turn heat to low, cover and cook for 15 minutes.

Meanwhile, bring a large pot of water to a boil over high heat. Stir in 1 Tablespoon salt. Break pasta in half and add to boiling water. Stir constantly for 1 minute so pasta doesn't stick together. Cook for about 8 minutes or until tasted done. Strain pasta in a colander and add to sauce mixture. Stir to combine. Top with cheddar cheese.

SESAME CORN BISCUITS

½ cup yellow cornmeal
1 ½ cups flour
½ teaspoon salt
4 teaspoons baking powder
½ teaspoon cream of tartar
2 Tablespoons sugar
½ cup butter
2/3 cup milk
Milk & sesame seeds

Preheat oven to 425°. Cover a large baking sheet with foil and grease with cooking spray. In a large mixing bowl, measure cornmeal, flour, salt, baking powder, cream of tartar and sugar. Cut butter into small pieces and mix into flour with your fingers, until it resembles fine crumbs. Stir in milk until combined. Place dough on a floured surface and pat into an 8" square, about ½" thick. Cut dough into 16 squares with a knife.

Place squares on prepared baking sheet and brush biscuits with a little milk. Sprinkle with sesame seeds. Bake for 15 minutes, until golden brown. Serve hot with butter. (Makes 16 biscuits)

STRAWBERRY ANGEL CAKE

1 baked angel food cake
1 (3.4 oz) pkg. instant vanilla pudding mix
1 (8 oz) can crushed pineapple
1 (16 oz) carton Cool Whip, thawed
½ cup chopped pecans
1 pint fresh strawberries

Mark the cake with 4 toothpicks about 1 inch down from the top of the cake. Use a long serrated bread knife to gently cut off the top of the angel food cake, using the toothpicks as a guide. Reserve top of cake. Use a smaller knife to cut a tunnel in the bottom part of the cake, being careful not to cut all the way through the cake's bottom and sides, leaving a shell of at least 1" on sides and bottom. Scoop out cake carefully (Remember to eat this left over cake!)

In a medium size bowl, mix together dry pudding mix and pineapple with the juice. Measure 1 cup Cool Whip and gently stir into bowl and add pecans.

Remove 6 whole strawberries and set aside. Wash, hull and slice remaining strawberries and add to filling.

Spoon filling into tunnel. Place top of cake back on filled cake. Frost cake with remaining Cool Whip (top first, then outside, then inside). Wash the 6 whole strawberries and decorate top of the cake with the whole strawberries. Refrigerate.

When ready to serve, slice cake with a serrated knife, using a sawing motion in order to keep from squashing the cake.

YOUNG EVERYDAY GOURMET

COCA-COLA CHICKEN

CHEESY POTATO CHUNKS

CHOCOLATE CHIP EXTRAVAGANZA

COCA-COLA CHICKEN

16 chicken breast tenders
Cavender's Greek seasoning
½ cup ketchup
½ cup Coca-Cola Classic
1 teaspoon Worcestershire sauce

Sprinkle chicken tenders with Cavender's seasoning on both sides. Grease a large non-stick skillet with Pam and place over medium high heat. When skillet is hot, add half the chicken tenders. Cook 5 minutes on each side, turning with tongs. Remove and repeat with the remaining chicken. Return all the chicken to the skillet and add ketchup, Coca-Cola and Worcestershire sauce. Heat until bubbly, about 5 minutes. Serve chicken with sauce spooned on top. (Serves 8)

CHEESY POTATO CHUNKS

12 small red potatoes
Salt & pepper to taste
¼ cup butter
1 cup grated cheddar cheese

Wash and scrub potatoes clean. Cut each potato into small chunks. Place in a medium size saucepan and add enough water to cover potatoes. Bring to a boil over high heat and cook until tender, about 10 minutes. Remove from heat and pour into a colander to drain off water. Place potatoes in a serving dish and add salt, pepper, butter and cheese. Stir gently to coat potatoes with seasonings. (Serves 8)

CHOCOLATE CHIP EXTRAVAGANZA

½ cup butter
½ cup sugar
½ cup light brown sugar
½ teaspoon vanilla
1 egg
1 ½ cups flour
½ cup semisweet chocolate chips

TOPPINGS:
¼ cup chocolate chips
¼ cup peanut butter chips
¼ cup white chocolate chips
¼ cup mini marshmallows
¼ cup M & M's

Preheat oven to 350°. Take butter out of refrigerator to soften before using (or heat in the microwave on high for about 10 seconds, until soft but not melted).

In a large mixing bowl combine butter, sugar, brown sugar, vanilla and egg. Mix well with a spoonula or a wooden spoon. Add flour and stir until a soft dough forms and flour is combined. Stir in chocolate chips.

Grease a 12 inch pizza pan with Pam and press dough evenly in the pan, forming a rim around the edge with your fingers. Bake for 15 minutes, remove from oven and sprinkle with toppings. Lightly press toppings down into dough with a spatula. Return pan to the oven for about 5 minutes, just until marshmallows start to melt. Remove from oven and let cool completely in pan. Cut into wedges to serve. (Makes 12 servings)

INDEX

A

B

C

D

E

F

G

H

I

J

L

M

N

O

P

Q

R

S

T

U

V

W

Z

NOTES

NOTES

NOTES

NOTES

Made in the USA
Lexington, KY
19 September 2014